LAWN WARS

Also by Lois B. Robbins:

Waking Up in the Age of Creativity

LAWN WARS:

THE STRUGGLE FOR A NEW LAWN ETHIC

BY

LOIS B. ROBBINS

iUniverse, Inc.
New York   Bloomington

Lawn Wars
The struggle for New Lawn Ethic

iUniverse books may be ordered through booksellers or by contacting:

iUniverse
1663 Liberty Drive
Bloomington, IN 47403
www.iuniverse.com
1-800-Authors (1-800-288-4677)

*Because of the dynamic nature of the Internet, any Web addresses or links
contained in this book may have changed since publication and may no longer be
valid. The views expressed in this work are solely those of the author and do not
necessarily reflect the views of the publisher, and the publisher hereby disclaims
any responsibility for them.*

ISBN: 978-1-4401-2351-1 (pbk)
ISBN: 978-1-4401-2352-8 (ebk)

Printed in the United States of America

Photo of Green baby was contributed by Jan Martin.

iUniverse rev. date: 3/6/2009

Table of Contents

Acknowledgements

It could take another book to name and thank all the people who have had some part, wittingly or unwittingly, in the writing of *Lawn Wars*. So I'll just hit the highlights. There are my parents, who instilled in me a love of the natural world. And there are old friends, like Diane Hoagland and Jean McIntire, who encouraged me in my earliest gardening efforts. And there are my good neighbors, Tom and Cindy Thebo, who haven't reported me to the township authorities even though they have to look at my unconventional landscaping every day.

Probably the most enduring influence has been that of Sara Stein, the author *Noah's Garden*, the reading of which opened floodgates in my mind. Author Michael Pollan's unique perspective on humankind's relationship with the natural world opened other floodgates.

Later, Trish Hennig, the owner of *American Roots*, a local native plant nursery, whose passion for native landscaping is contagious, got me to join our local chapter of *Wild Ones* where I learned enough to feel like I know what I'm talking about. I owe enormous gratitude to Ruth Vrbensky, who owns *Oakland Wildflower Farm*, another local native plant nursery. Ruth and I, natural landscaper Celia Ryker, and wildlife biologist Rick McAvinchey, formed the dirt-under-the-fingernails-sweat-on-the-brow team who worked together on three native landscape demonstration projects in our village. The impetus for those projects came from The Oakland Native Partnership Initiative (ONPI) and local businesses who funded them. I shouldn't leave out Dave Green, who organized Four-H kids to help us. Huge thanks to Fred Waybrant and Brent Blackburn, who laid thousands of bricks for our *Heritage Garden* walkways. All have earned my deepest gratitude and admiration for their spunk, their expertise, and their indefatigable determination to bring our projects to completion.

I also want to thank the ONPI partners, whose help extended far beyond the funding of our projects: The North Oakland Headwaters Land Conservancy, Friends of the Rouge, The Clinton River Watershed Council, Oakland County Planning and Economic Development Services, with special thanks to Nina Ignaczek and Erin Lavender, the Oakland Chapter of Wild Ones, with special thanks to Maryann Whitman, and the Oakland Land Conservancy, with special thanks to Donna Folland. The County's map guys, Jim Keglovitz, Larry Falardeau, and Kristen Wiltfang have helped me understand the Big Picture.

Certainly Bill Schneider, owner of *Wild Type* native plant nursery, has had an important role in educating me about lawn alternatives. Naturalist and nature writer, Jonathan Schechter helped with some information on invasive species. Gail mally mack, Nancy Nordlie, Jan Robbins, and Gary Woodward, gave the manuscript the once over and provided feedback. My son, Bill Robbins held my hand through my steep computer learning curve.

In the same way that I'm indebted to Sara Stein and Michael Pollan, I'm also greatly indebted to Jens Jensen, a true pioneer and prophet of the natural landscaping movement, and to Robert Grese at the University of Michigan's School of Natural Resources. Without his extensive research for his moving book, Jens *Jensen: Maker of Natural Parks and Gardens,* Chapters 10 and 11 would not exist. And finally, I'd like to thank Cat Mandu, for keeping my lap warm through the entire writing of this book.

INTRODUCTION

Elk War

When Joel and Eva moved into their new home on a Colorado mountaintop, they wisely installed a xeriscape, landscaping their property with plants indigenous to the area. Their neighbor, also moving into a new house, shaved off all the existing vegetation and covered his nine acres with sod. Joel and Eva thought the neighbor's lawn looked ridiculous in a Rocky Mountain evergreen forest, a place where lawn grasses would never grow on their own. Apparently the elk thought so too, for they moved in as well, (or refused to move out), and had a field day with the newly laid sod, pawing it, picking it up, and tossing it around with abandon. When the neighbors returned home that evening, they found their new lawn in a shambles. War was declared on the elk.

Why would anyone put a lawn in a place like this? The reasons are many and varied, reflecting our American passion for open spaces and our notions of land ownership and gentry.

History and Image

Picture this: An unimpeded expanse of green, rolling gently toward a Greek-Revival antebellum plantation home. Graceful willow trees arch over a blacktopped driveway that curves gently toward the columned entryway to the main house, the epitome of gracious living. Advertisers often use images such as this to emphasize the quality of their product (usually a car) and the wealth it denotes. Although you don't see the serfs or slaves of times past, or the employees that even today are required to keep a place like this going, the implication is that the owner of this property (and car) is a personage of power, an ipso-facto slave owner.

This image is so thoroughly engraved in the American psyche that many Americans will go to almost any length to present it as packaging for who they imagine themselves to be. Those of us who can afford it spend thousands of dollars on lawn service every year to maintain the image. Those who can't, spend every warm weekend mowing, blowing, edging, trimming, spraying, whacking, fertilizing, pulling heavy rollers to flatten hillocks, and dragging bags of grass clippings and leaves to the curb to be hauled off to an already overburdened landfill. Who's the slave here?

Not only will we go to any length to maintain our lawns, we will even take them with us to places where lawns don't normally exist, as Joel and Eva's neighbor did. During the World War II occupation of the Philippines, I heard about GIs whose job it was to cut the grass in front of the Major's house with scissors, since there were no lawn mowers there. Even there, the American lawn was painfully in evidence.

Not everyone wears their lawn with ostentation. For many it's simply a matter of doing what everybody else is doing. But there are lawns that cover many acres and do present the owner as a person of some means. I don't mean to imply that any of this is conscious. Some of the most socially conscious people I know have large lawns and tend them carefully. The idea that they are trying to appear like slave owners or landed gentry would be deeply offensive to them. Yet the image of the master of his domain, re-enforced by a large lawn, is indelibly tattooed on their unconscious, as, I confess, it is on mine, influencing many of their decisions.

It seems as if we've always had lawns. No one ever questioned it. With the advent of commercial petroleum-based fertilizers and chemical pesticides following the Second World War, lawn-keeping evolved into a high art for the average American, and the "grass farmer" (the householder who spends many off-the-job hours cultivating his lawn), was born.

I believe lawn owners, unconsciously hoping to emulate the Southern plantations or the estates of the noble lords of Medieval Europe, were anxious to show that "all this is mine." In the Feudal System, the estate, with its rolling landscape that was not needed for crops, was kept "mowed" either by herds of sheep, or by serfs whose job it was to scythe the tall grass down. The lawn became a symbol of wealth and power. It shouted to all passersby that this landowner is so wealthy that his serfs can be spared from the necessities of agriculture and utilized instead for beautification.

Harking back to the landed gentry with serfs to do their bidding, our European-American forebears, with some nostalgia for the world they'd left behind, incorporated these symbols into their collective psyche. They brought with them the grasses and medicinal herbs they'd known in their moist native land. These closely cropped grasses that had evolved along with the grazing sheep, goats and cows of their homeland, did not (and do not now) do well in the harsher climate of North America. They evolved with the prevailing fogs and drizzles of their region of origin. Without a great deal of care to simulate the conditions they evolved with in Europe, our lawns would languish. Their short roots cannot reach water in dry conditions. They are susceptible to many diseases for which they have not evolved adequate natural defenses.

Even the etymology of the word "lawn" reflects this influence, rooted as it is in the word, *laund*, which means *heath*. A *heath* is an area of open land typically found in England and Scotland that is overgrown with coarse herbage. The word *heathen* also comes from this root, and originally referred to people who live on the heath, just as *pagan* originally meant the agrarian people of the countryside. Later *heathen* came to mean the common people, who, like the heathers they lived among, tended to be wild, rough, and "unchristian".

One can only speculate on the extent to which we also incorporated the notion of wild, uncultivated land as synonymous with unchristian as well. Our word *lawn* has managed to turn *laund* on its head, and now refers to a highly cultivated and neatly tended open space. Although appearing wealthy is not always the reason for having a lawn, nostalgia usually is.

Nostalgia runs deep and wide. Maybe you remember, as I do, high top boots, which, along with knickers, were all the rage for young boys during the late '30's and early '40's. My brother wore them and I coveted them. They had a little pocket at the top, near the knee, where a jack knife was kept. Of what use were these high boots and jack knives to boys who lived in cities where there was no mud, no cow-pies, no tall grass, and no vines to cut through? None.

It was what these boots symbolized that made them popular. I realized this watching a TV documentary on the contemporary English nobility. There was the proper English gentleman in his ascot, knickers, and tweed jacket with patched elbows, out in his pasture where, since he had no serfs as he might have had in former days, he probably did need those high-top boots with a jack-knife in the pocket. When I saw the knickers and the boots, exactly like the ones my brother wore, I saw in a flash, the way such nostalgias manifest in popular culture.

The lawn represents another nostalgic image as well. We pine for the open spaces of the West and the Midwestern prairies: "Oh give me a home where the buffalo roam, and don't fence me in," it says. "I'm master of my fate, and I have dominion over this land." "This land is my land . . ."

In the 1870's Frederick Law Olmsted, the man who designed New York's Central Park, referred to the lawn as "the great democratizer." For him, the lack of fences, the seamlessness of a large expanse of lawn, symbolized access for all, and was the antithesis of The Feudal *Enclosure*, when peasants were excluded from feudal estates except for their labor.

For city dwellers, the lawn often represents their last small connection with the natural world, a mini-escape from civilization. Now it has become a symbol of the very civilization from which one might like to escape.

The American lawn didn't really get a stranglehold on the American psyche until after World War II, when the *GI Bill of Rights* made home ownership possible to thousands of vets. Before then, the notion of the colonial garden, a carry-over from the English Cottage Garden, still competed with large expanses of turf for American affection. With World War II came the advent of chemicals and petroleum fertilizers that made grass-farming possible. Thanks to GI loans, the suburbs that proliferated across the United States firmly established the American lawn as an icon. There are other reasons for its popularity as well.

Vista

I stand at the living room window in my daughter's house in New Jersey. The lawn slopes away, clean and uncluttered, down to a small copse of sumac. Beyond that, her neighbor's lawn sweeps downward toward a lush valley. Occasional houses dot the hillsides beyond, and silhouettes of cows make smaller dots beyond. The horizon is held by hills that are almost mountains, their solid blue curvilinear forms rising against the sky. It pleases my eye. My daughter has a view. A vista. A view is worth a lot in terms of real estate, and people will pay dearly to have one.

Standing in my daughter's window, I understand why. I feel like I'm on top of the world. Troubles melt away as the distant blue hills draw my eye deeper into the landscape. It's not simply a longer than usual perspective *out there* that I'm looking at. I'm experiencing a larger perspective *in here* as well. Looking at such a scene literally "puts things in perspective." Our concerns and preoccupations are shown for the trivialities they mostly are.

Ponder the word *vista*. What are its psychological implications? What is it in the human soul that desires vista? Why will we sometimes travel some distance out of our way to find a "lookout" where we can see for miles and miles?

We are awestruck by a panoramic view from the mountains. Our souls are laid bare when we see a green valley stretched out at our feet. Metaphorically, to "see" means to *comprehend*. When we look at such a scene, we do seem to comprehend more, possibly because there's more there to be comprehended. Perhaps we feel comforted by knowing, as our stone-age ancestors undoubtedly did when viewing such a scene, that no predator could sneak up without our knowing it. Perhaps the green valley represents a genetically imprinted reassurance that there will be enough to eat. Where there is green there is water and there is life.

Landscape designers often use the term "prospect-refuge" and strive to create them in a landscape. A *prospect-refuge* is a somewhat enclosed space from which to view a vista. Landscapers recognize that such spaces provide a comfort-zone for humans - possibly for other animals as well, ones that evolved in a savanna environment, a safe place from which to survey the landscape for possible predators or prey. It's probable that our desire for *vista*, or *prospect-refuge* is encoded in our DNA.

The Funk & Wagnalls Dictionary gives us another clue. It says that to "see" is to have a "mental view, embracing a series of events." As a verb, to *see* means to have the care and supervision of, attend, care for, look after, mind, minister, tend, watch. It calls forth our yearning to nurture. We need these spaces, and on some deep level we know we are called to care for them. They need us as well, and caring for them brings us health and happiness. Deeper than appearances, the green lawn speaks to our desire to extend our care, to reciprocate for that which is given.

These are compelling reasons that to some extent explain the reluctance of most Americans to consider an alternative. But they are fading in importance as new insights and information become available.

A New Enclosure

Part and parcel with the dramatic changes that are taking place worldwide as the *democratization of everything* continues to reach into every nook and cranny of our psyche, the dry husks of a romanticized past are dropping away. We no longer have or want slaves or serfs. Even the wealthiest and most powerful among us have to pay their servants a living wage. Are we willing to *be* slaves? Are we willing to subject wild animals to slavery? Are we creating a new "enclosure" as the gentry of the Middle Ages did? When the gentry fenced off large tracts of land, they did so to enclose the wild animals *within* their property so that they could be hunted for the lord's dinner table. Now we are *excluding* animals from our property, and from our consciousness. And we are simultaneously degrading the fragments of wildlife habitat that remain, in some cases causing the extinction of the animals that depend on them.

Soul

The problem is that every time we plant a lawn, we delete several entries from the local wildlife database. We delete our own craving for wildness as well. Wild places possess mystery and harmony for which our souls yearn. The loss of these habitats is a loss not only to the animals whose lives depend on them, but to our own souls as well.

We need these other life forms for more than meat, or for the role they play in ecological balance. By excluding these other life forms from our consciousness, we are bringing about a debilitation and diminishment of the human spirit. We *need* these other life forms, the beauty they express and the delight with which they enrich our lives. They help to define who we are. Without them our lives are sterile, as we narcissistically try to convince ourselves that humans are the only species that matter.

Habits and images are hard to change, as property owners who are trying to change are finding out. These habits have mythological origins. They are deeply rooted in beliefs that were never questioned. But now, more and more people *are* questioning them, and are looking for alternatives to the time-honored lawn. I count myself among them. We are coming to view the American lawn as an ecological catastrophe. It's a hard sell. People love their lawns and won't easily give them up.

But our love affair with the lawn is drawing to a close. Driving down any suburban street, it may not look this way yet, but in fundamental ways, it's over. Just as a relationship can carry on in diminished capacity long before a divorce is initiated, we are slowly waking up to the insupportability of the American lawn. Rumblings foretell its eventual demise.

My intention here is to be a recruiter, to inspire others to kick their lawn addiction. I offer stories, encouragement, models, and practical suggestions to others who might be attracted to a different way of being with their property. The way of the new lawn ethic suggested here is less constricted by traditions and habits of thought, of whose sources we are only dimly aware. It is a way that is more generous, more in harmony with and willing to learn from the natural world. And I hope to awaken something much deeper than that: a sense of the sacredness that lies beneath our feet, a world of beauty and wonder that's waiting to be released from the chains of the industrial age.

PART I:

A New Lawn Ethic

CHAPTER 1:

It Seemed Like a Good Idea at the Time

Art gone to decay emphasizes the form only,
for the spirit has disappeared.

Jens Jensen, *Siftings*

A Desire for Change

The desire for change rumbles under the thin veneer of the American lawn, a longing to recover what was lost when we embraced its smooth seduction.

The sense of estrangement at the bottom of this restless desire for change arises from cultural notions about the place of the human in the cosmos, and reveals a deep tension between nature and culture that has been with us for at least 200 years, perhaps longer. It's one of the tensions that have brought this situation about. Other tensions arising from this Great Divide include:

-Common Vs. private ownership
-Petroleum-based fertilizers Vs. composting
-Chemical pesticides Vs. organic agriculture
-Biodiversity Vs. monoculture
-Exotic Vs. native species

These tensions have often been resolved by decisions that were later regretted. How many of the "up-to-date" practices we enthusiastically embrace today will turn out to have been worse than if we'd done nothing at all?

I won't go so far as to suggest, as some have done, that *the cause of problems is solutions,* but I do think our rashness as a species is undergoing some kind of tempering as we discover how difficult it is to live with the consequences of many of our "bright" ideas. Bioregionalist Stephanie Mills believes the mantra of the 20th century has been, *It seemed like a good idea at the time.* As we survey the various difficulties we've brought upon ourselves, we can see that in every case, it *did* seem like a good idea at the time. Negative consequences have frequently issued from our ignorance of long-term effects on natural systems that were functioning well until we interfered with them.

Common and Private Ownership

Tensions between private and public or communal ownership have existed since before the beginning of recorded history. Before European settlement, the natives of the North American continent held their lands in common. The idea of private ownership of land, an artifact of the feudal system, was incomprehensible to them, as it is to contemporary indigenous populations around the world. Chief Seattle put it well:

> How can you buy or sell the sky, the warmth of the land? The idea is strange to us. If we do not own the freshness of the air and the sparkle of the water, how can you buy them? . . .
> We know that the white man does not understand our ways.
> One portion of land is the same to him as the next, for he is a stranger who comes in the night and takes from the land whatever he needs. The earth is not his brother, but his enemy, and when he has conquered it, he moves on.

The notion of the commons, the European idea of land that was owned by everybody, had its origins in ancient Greece and found its fullest expression in The *Public Trust Doctrine*, which gave birth to our constitution. First appearing in Roman law, then later in English Common Law, the *Public Trust Doctrine* establishes public ownership of certain natural resources and underlies modern environmental law. It states that the public owns common or shared environments - air, waters, dunes, tidelands, underwater lands, fisheries, shellfish beds, parks and commons, and migratory species, and in some cases, sacred sites and historical monuments. The value of these systems is to be maintained for all users, including future generations. Government trustees are responsible for looking after them. These public trust rights cannot be extinguished, because they are said to derive from "natural" or God-given law.

In their book, *The Riverkeepers*, Robert Kennedy, Jr. and John Cronin explore the origins of American democracy, showing that the Magna Carta, from which we draw our Bill of Rights, grew out of a revolt of the European common people brought about by the enclosure.[1] Later codified in English Common Law, from which many of our own laws were crafted, the Magna Carta, rested on *The Public Trust Doctrine*. This was then woven into the U.S. Bill of Rights. Kennedy and Cronin note: "Following the American Revolution, each state became sovereign, with trusteeship of public lands and waters and wildlife within its borders."[2]

In the U.S., where individualism and private property are held sacrosanct, there has always been tension between lands and waterways held in public trust and private ownership. Often these tensions erupt in epic battles played out in township halls across the country. People move to the country, as I did, to escape the congestion and environmental degradation of the city and suburbs. Once I arrived in my country place, I, like my neighbors who would have liked to keep *me* out, wanted to shut the door behind me. "OK, now. That's enough people here. We don't need any more," we'd like to have said. We knew that more people would mean the loss of the very thing we came here for, - the low-density population, the rural character of the area, the closeness to nature, the quiet. But strive as we might to keep them out, after a while the suburbs are transplanted to areas that were formerly farmland and wildlife habitat.

Many property owners fight environmental legislation on the grounds that these laws will interfere with the rights of private ownership of property. Many of these same people, illogically, will vigorously defend zoning laws that also impinge on the rights of private ownership. These fights are very real and often result in weaker environmental laws and certain setback ordinances that make it difficult for homeowners who wish to establish backyard wildlife habitat, or who just want a more natural looking landscape.

Other tensions are affecting our life-spaces as well. These have to do with the tensions over water conservation, fertilizer runoff, pesticides, and species extinction.

Environmental Degradation

So here goes the inevitable litany. The part you probably don't want to read and I'd rather not have to write. This is the part about how the American lawn epitomizes our war with nature. Some things you'd rather not know. This is one of them.

Water Conservation and Diversion

It seemed like a good idea at the time. In the post-war years engineers became adept at damming rivers for power generation. Vast networks of reservoirs and aqueducts were built to bring water to places that had previously been uninhabitable. In some places, they caused the desert to bloom, a feat which was heralded as a technological miracle. It also made lawns possible in areas where they shouldn't be.

Lawns are about surfaces. Their roots are shallow. Most lawns are so dense that much of the rainwater that might nourish their shallow roots runs off into storm sewers and eventually to lakes and streams, carrying with it fertilizers and pesticides. In the Southwest, it never gets that far, most of the water evaporating before it hits the ground. Attempts to recreate the American Lawn in desert areas can be quite pathetic. To keep these lawns green, water must be transported hundreds of miles. This often leads to some pretty irrational schemes, such as diversion of water from the Great Lakes, as was seriously considered a decade ago and continues to rear its head whenever things get tough in the desert.

The Great Lakes Commission, a collaboration between eight States and two Canadian provinces that border the Great Lakes, was first created to thwart threats such as these, as well as the environmental damage that would result from such tampering with the greatest source of fresh water in the Western hemisphere. In September, 2008, a compact between the eight Great Lakes states and two Canadian provinces was ratified by the U. S. Congress. As shortages of clean water become more critical, ways will likely be found to challenge this compact.

With their truncated root systems, the lawns we are addicted to require enormous amounts of water to keep them green. Not a problem in earlier years when fresh water seemed to be in inexhaustible supply. Now, with the pollution of our waterways and aquifers, clean, fresh water is rapidly becoming a vanishing resource. The time is probably not far off when major battles will be fought over water, in this country as well as in the Middle East.

There are other tensions involved in environmental degradation as well. The evil twins in this melodrama are petroleum-based fertilizers and chemical pesticides.

Fertilizers

It seemed like a good idea at the time. When petroleum-based fertilizers first hit the marketplace, my father delighted in telling the story of his friend, Milt, who ridiculed the idea, convinced that unfertilized grass would be just as green as grass that had been fertilized. In the dark of night, Dad sneaked over to Milt's house with several bags of fertilizer and a spreader. While Milt slept, Dad meticulously wrote his initials, SWB, in giant letters on Milt's front lawn. As the weeks went by, the rich dark green SWB stood out more and more until Milt got the message: Fertilizer works. It's odorless, easy to buy and use, and makes lawns look great. Soon Milt and thousands of Americans were pouring tons of it on their lawns. Animal manure, compost, and "green manure" from used cover crops proved too costly to manufacture in quantity. Petroleum, then a cheap and abundant resource, began to be used as a primary source of fertilizer, by lawn owners and by farmers.

Petroleum-based fertilizers have worked so well for lawns and golf courses, as well as for agriculture, that it is now a seventeen billion dollar industry. Lawns account for 25 percent of profits for this industry.[3] It took a while before enough of the runoff from these chemically fertilized lawns got into lakes and streams to cause damage. It was longer still before the effects of this became visible, with lakes and wetlands filling in with vegetation, (eutrophying), far faster than their natural rate.

We became alarmed in the '70s when Lake Erie was pronounced "dead", largely as a result of accelerated eutrophication nourished by fertilizer runoff. Since that time, Lake Erie has made a decent recovery, but wetlands, lakes and waterways near subdivisions and golf courses continue to fight for breath.

In a 2001 study, Lake Tahoe was found to be "in danger of becoming a shallow shadow of its former self." The report's executive summary warns, "Lake Tahoe is gravely imperiled."[4] Lawn fertilizer was found to be at the root of the problem, along with diesel exhaust and crumbling road banks.

Pesticides

One day many years ago, before the publication of *Silent Spring,* a child appeared at my door with a grotesquely dead robin. Our trees had just been sprayed, probably with DDT, for Dutch Elm Disease. *It seemed like a good idea at the time.*

I don't remember the conversation but the gist of the child's message was that the spray had killed the robin. "Nonsense!" I thought. I couldn't believe any practice so widely encouraged could have so deleterious an effect. It took a long time before I could admit to myself, if not to the child, that I had, in effect, killed the robin by ordering the spraying. It took another 40 years for Americans to accept the horrible truth that that same act (and others like it) might well have been the one that put DDT into the breast milk our babies want and need.

Since the end of World War II, we've been waging a massive war against the natural world. With the best of intentions, we've been fighting a Civil War, both with nature "out there," and in here, with our own human nature. Though not immediately visible, the results of this war have been devastating both to the natural world on which our own lives depend, and to our sense of inner peace. We are a house divided against itself.

As individuals, we wage this war most intensely in our own homes and properties. With an impressive arsenal of herbicides, insecticides, pesticides, we have imposed our scorched-earth policy on every other creature that is trying to make a living in our vicinity. And we are coming to realize, late in this war, that our own weapons are turning against us. It doesn't require sophisticated espionage to discover the basic way this has come about. The code is right there before our eyes, in our own everyday language. The code is the combining form, "-cide": Insecti*cide*. Herbi*cide*. Pesti*cide*. Fungi*cide*. Homi*cide*. Geo*cide*.

Funk & Wagnall's tells us that -*cide* is a combining form meaning "killer, or destroyer, or murderer, stemming from the Latin root, cida, killer; cidium, slaughter." Anything with -*cide* in it is intended to kill. The problem is that -*cides* seldom differentiate amongst their victims. If they can kill a bug they can also kill a dog. Or a bird. Or a human. The -*cide* doesn't go away just because a bug has eaten it. Whatever eats the bug also eats the -*cide*, as we learned from Rachel Carson in the '60's. It's the story of the old lady who swallowed the fly. She died, of course. It's as if, right in the middle of bombing Iraq, we suddenly turned our smart bombs and missiles toward ourselves. To make matters worse, the -*cide* becomes more concentrated and more lethal the farther up the food-chain it travels. And we are at the top.

Let's take a mouse. You may have any one of the many that find their way into my house every fall. You've been engaged in a rapidly escalating military buildup with this mouse, starting with the merciful Victor live-trap, releasing into your neighbor's field the mice that haven't escaped by chewing through the trap's plastic, hoping your neighbor won't figure out what you're doing, perhaps even noting that at the same time, your neighbor is releasing *her* mice onto *your* property. (This is now illegal in some areas where the rule is that you must kill whatever you trap.)

But you still hear mice when you're trying to sleep. Then, escalating to the spring trap, you've been revolted by the small broken body you had to dispose of. Finally, determined to win this war and stop the scritching between the walls next to your bed, you offer the mouse a tasty meal of D-Con, containing Brodifacoum, a powerful pesticide. Wonderful! You don't have to deal with the results at all. You don't have to drive a mile to your neighbor's field. You don't have to be sickened by removing a mutilated mouse body from the spring trap. You never even see the mouse. She's just gone, and so are the baby mice she took it home to.

It's been a surgical strike and you've won this war. But while you're enjoying a peaceful night's sleep without any mouse-scritching in the walls next to your bed, there's another drama being played out. The mouse dies outside, where it has gone to seek water to slake the unbearable thirst brought on by the D-Con. If an owl or your cat gets the mouse, or one of the mouse's babies who have also enjoyed this lethal meal, the owl or cat will also die. Even if the mouse is not eaten, its little body still carries the persistent chemical that killed it. If it isn't eaten, the mouse decays, and the chemical is carried into the soil that was the deceased mouse's death bed. From there, the chemical eventually finds its way into the source of your drinking water. In other words, while you are killing the mouse, you are also killing yourself or your progeny. Or if the poison finds its way into a lake or stream, it may find its way into the fish you eat. You've won the battle but lost the war. Remember, the further up the food-chain the poison moves, the more concentrated it becomes in the fatty tissue, where it can cause cancer.

And so it goes with the stuff you spray on your roses, the herbicides you or your lawn service apply to your lawn, or the chemical insecticide you spray on the vegetables in your garden that you will eventually eat. You don't believe a lawn service would use anything that could be harmful to humans? In her groundbreaking book, *Living Downstream*, Sandra Steingraber cites a 1995 Denver study: "children whose yards were treated with pesticides were four times more likely to have soft tissue cancers than children living in households that did not use yard chemicals."[5] In another study, it was found that "the risk of canine malignant lymphoma doubles with four or more 2,4-D applications per year on a dog owner's lawn."[6] Reinforcing our suspicions, we learn that, according to an occupational study, "golf course superintendents die more often from cancer than the general population."[7] Although the Environmental Protection Agency now regulates 2,4-D in drinking water, as of September, 2008 the EPA had not classified 2,4-D as to its human carcinogenicity, stating that *there is no evidence that bioconcentration of 2,4-D occurs through the food chain.*[8]

The Garden Club of America has noted that 67 million pounds of pesticides are used on American lawns every year. That's 11% of all U. S. pesticide use, according to Dennis Van Engles in a recent TED Talk. Steingraber reminds us, "Yard and garden weed killers are used by about 50 percent of U. S. families, as are insecticidal flea collars, sprays, dusts, shampoos, and dips for household pets."[9] All of these contain pesticides, the harmfulness of which has yet to be determined. Why? Because "two thirds of the most widely used chemicals have still not gone through basic carcinogenicity tests."[10]

Surely the products you use on your gardens and your pets are safe, you think. Surely they wouldn't be allowed on the market if they weren't. Think again. A June 23, 1993 Newsweek article stated that at that time, only two of the 34 major lawn care pesticides had been tested for their long-term effects on humans and the environment.

A 2003 Environment and Human Health, Inc. (EHHI) report, *Risks from Lawn Care Pesticides*, states, "Consumers presume that lawn-care pesticides are safe because they are sold in stores that also market foods and other consumer products. Products such as 'Weed-and Feed,' 'Weed-B-Gon,' and 'Turf Builder with PLUS2 Weed Control' are all names that might seem innocuous to the consumer, but they contained pesticides such as 2,4-D, which has been linked to non-Hodgkin's lymphoma, and MCPP, which has been associated with soft tissue cancers. Products such as 'Bug-B-Gone' and 'Turf Builder with Insect Control' also might sound quite benign to the consumer, but they contain carbaryl and diazinon, both of which are capable of harming the nervous system." Carbaryl, currently classified by the USEPA as acceptable for general use, is suspected of altering human hormone function and may be implicated in the collapse of honey bee populations.[11] Recognizing diazinon, an organophosphate insecticide, as a special threat to children, the United States Environmental Protection Agency (USEPA) phased out its residential use in 2004. MCPP (Mecoprop-p) is currently under review by the USEPA. As of this writing, however 2,4-D still remains a key ingredient in most pesticides sold for residential use.

The Northwest Coalition for Alternatives to Pesticides reports that the four most commonly used pesticides in U. S. backyards, diazinon (Knox-out or Spectracide), propoxur(Baygon), chlorpyrifos (Dursban), and carbaryl (Sevin) are nerve poisons that cause muscle weakness, headaches, nausea, and incoordination. Although dursban and diazinon have been banned for residential use, the others, as of this writing, are still on the market.

Pesticides. There's that combining form, *-cide* again. Whenever you see that combining form, you know it's something that can kill just about anything. Most of the chemicals that have been banned from production are the ones that have been proven to cause cancer. That leaves out a whole spectrum of chemicals like propoxur and carbaryl that may cause nerve damage and genetic breakdown. For example, In a July 28, 2006 National Public Radio program, Dan Gunderson of Minnesota Public Radio cited preliminary research at the University of North Dakota that suggests a link between pesticides and both Alzheimers and Parkinson Diseases. These are not cancers, but brain disorders. Besides diseases commonly attributed to old age, the use of these neurotoxins can result in lowered sperm counts, blurred genders, and genetic learning and behavioral disorders. A June 19, 2000 article in U. S. News and World Report states: ". . . neurotoxicants and (their effect on) genes may account for nearly 24 percent of developmental problems. There are 850 known neurotoxicants, any of which 'may result in devastating neurological or psychiatric disorders that impair the quality of life, cripple and potentially reduce the highest intellect to a vegetative state." Although these may or may not cause cancer, and hence many have not been banned, they are deeply implicated in the disruption of normal hormone function.

Even though some chemicals may no longer be made in the U. S., the ones that were made before they were banned are still in the air, water, soil, and in the fatty tissue of every human and every other living thing on the planet, even in Antarctica. Steingraber notes that Triazines, commonly used on lawns, "have been detected in raindrops in twenty-three states in the upper Midwest and the Northeast, including pristine areas such as Isle Royale National Park . . . It is known that triazines inhibit the growth of native prairie species. Like corn, mature plants are tolerant of the herbicides, but seedlings are quite susceptible".[12] Despite these concerns, a 2006 EPA Fact Sheet states, "with the mitigation measures in the individual atrazine and simazine decisions, cumulative risks are below EPA's FQPA regulatory level of concern." Altrazine and simazine are both in a class of chemicals called triazines, the ones that have shown up in rainwater everywhere and are a threat to native plant species. The reasons for concern about their affect on native plants will become clear in Part II.

Other countries still make chemicals banned in the U. S. and use them to treat many of the foods we import and eventually eat. While some foreign countries are ahead of us in banning harmful chemicals, many still depend on them for crop-yields. A decade ago, when Hudson, Quebec, banned the use of chemical herbicides and insecticides on lawns, the town was sued by landscaping companies *ChemLawn* and *Spraytech*. Following many appeals, "In June, 2001, the Canadian Supreme Court upheld the town's right to ban pesticides, based on the *precautionary principle*."[13] The *precautionary principle* asks that a company prove a product is safe before it can be used. Now, many local governments in Canada and elsewhere are invoking this principle to protect their citizens.

Despite this progress, international agreements have made it difficult for some countries to enact the legislation they've adopted to protect the health of their citizens. In 2001 a major U.S. manufacturer of the pesticide *lindane* filed a $100 million lawsuit against Canada under the North American Free Trade Agreement (NAFTA) for banning the chemical they manufacture, even though its use is banned in the U.S. The basis of the lawsuit was a NAFTA provision granting "private investors and corporations the right to sue NAFTA governments for damages if they feel that their investments have been hurt by national laws or regulations."[14] *Lindane*, currently being phased out in Europe after the E.U. banned it for all agricultural and horticultural uses in 2000, has been documented to cause dizziness, seizure, nervous system damage, immune system damage and birth defects. In 2006, the USEPA withdrew lindane from all agricultural uses in the United States, and in 2007 all lindane USEPA registrations were cancelled. Governments around the world are now moving to add lindane to the list of chemicals targeted for a global ban under the Stockholm Convention, but to date, the lindane lawsuit against Canada is unresolved.

Despite hopeful global progress, the Summer, 2006 Journal of Pesticide Reform reports: many chemicals once thought to be "safe" are still being made and used in the U.S. "Many pesticide ingredients are both untested and unidentified."[15]

It's not just the application of these *-cides* that causes the problem. How they and their manufacturing by-products combine with other chemicals in the environment can also be blamed. In her 1996 book on hormone disruptors, *Our Stolen Future*, Dr. Theo Colborn warns, "Never assume a pesticide is safe. Anything that kills pests can kill humans."[16]

Our war on nature is backfiring on us in other ways as well. While we've been gleefully overkilling everything in sight, including many insects that are beneficial, the very insects, microbes and viruses we've been attacking have been busily redoubling *their* defenses through the last mechanism available to them: evolution. Stronger and stronger strains have been quietly evolving since we fired the first *-cide* after World War II. Now it takes a great deal *more* toxins to kill many strains that were defeated easily in the early stages of this war.

"Addiction" equates with self-destructive behavior that requires more and more of the addictive substance to maintain a feeling of well-being. It seems clear that American society has a chemical addiction.

Mowers

> There is no quiet place in the white man's cities. No place
> to hear the unfurling of leaves in spring, or the rustle of
> insect's wings. But perhaps it is because I am a savage
> and do not understand. (Chief Seattle)

When the first mechanical mower was invented in 1850, it probably didn't bother anyone much. With the advent of the internal combustion engine, mowers became more noticeable. Today, it's unusual *not* to hear lawn mowers during every weekend daylight hour. Although the noise pollution from power mowers and weed-whackers doesn't seem to be on anyone's radar screen yet, it probably will be soon. In the past week, I've heard four conversations about "lawn etiquette," where the theme was, if you know your neighbor is barbecuing, don't mow your lawn. Some strictly controlled neighborhoods have designated hours when it is hoped everyone will be mowing so the neighborhood can be quiet the rest of the time. But the weather doesn't always cooperate with such good intentions. Nor does the need to control pollution. Ozone Action days, when mowing is actively discouraged in order to control smog, may be in conflict either with designated hours, or the dry, sunny times that are ideal for mowing.

A better solution is not to mow at all. Jaws drop when this is suggested, until it is learned that "A gasoline-powered mower spews out as much smog-forming gases as 30 average cars in one hour."[17] (Other sources say 50 cars!) These "smog-forming gases" include the dreaded hydrocarbons that are believed to be the cause of global warming and climate change.

Species Extinction and Loss of Habitat

Today in America, according to Herbert Muschamp, "over 32 million acres are covered with turfgrass."[18] That's over 40,000 square miles, more land than is cultivated for corn or wheat, and that figure is growing exponentially. Even taking into account the large number of golf courses and government and corporate "power lawns," (huge lawns maintained on corporate headquarters' property), the rate at which America is being turfed over is astonishing. Lawns are monocultures, with only one or two grass species represented. In Europe, they are called "green deserts," areas that look green, but harbor no genetic diversity. With so much land being turfed over, it doesn't leave much room for other kinds of flora or for wildlife habitat.

Both plant and animal species are facing extinction at a rate which far exceeds their natural comings and goings. On an unimaginable order of magnitude, species are disappearing from the face of the earth, never to be seen again. Loss of habitat is the primary reason, followed by the introduction of invasive exotic species (often stuff we plant in our gardens), as we shall see later. *It seemed like a good idea at the time.*

CHAPTER 2:

Lawn Sculpting

> I have had great joy
> in forming simple compositions
> with this living green.
>
> Jens Jensen, *Siftings*

Regrets

Wittingly or unwittingly, we've been at war with the natural world. On the one hand, we've won the war. On the other hand, we're beginning to comprehend the pervasive and insidious ways this mutually assured destruction may lead to our own defeat. If other species crash, unraveling the web of life, we'll crash as well. Our demise will be traceable to our own enthusiasm in our war against the natural world. What can we tell our children? How can we explain this to our grandchildren? How can we face them?

It seemed like a good idea at the time. The statement is full of regret and testimony to shortsightedness. Our culture has made many mistakes and the lawn is only one of them. We can assuage our guilt somewhat by understanding that we didn't know any better. But by what excuse can we now continue in these destructive habits?

There may have been a time when the war with nature was justified, when settlers in the New World had to defend themselves against predators and carve out places to grow food in a land covered with vast forests. But that war, the war with nature is over. We won. And now nature lies vanquished at our feet. James Hillman reminds

16

us that "Nature today is on dialysis, slowly expiring, kept alive only by advanced technology,"[19] We cannot hope to fix our broken world by doing more of what we did wrong in the first place. But merely stopping the wrong things will probably not be enough either. Have we painted ourselves into a corner where our most clever technologies will be required to extricate us from the mess we've created? Or can we just change, each of us, to practices more in harmony with natural systems? It will probably take a combination of both to pull us back from the brink of the destruction we've been causing.

A Quiet Rebellion

I heard about a man who installed a native prairie where his lawn had been. After he tore up his lawn, but before he planted it with native prairie species, friends and neighbors were invited to a funeral. With pomp and ceremony, he buried his lawn mower. While his lawn mower funeral might have been unique, this man is only one of many. A quiet rebellion is brewing. The lawn wars have begun. With any luck they will turn into a revolution. Although still not in any great numbers, many Americans are questioning this anachronism called the lawn.

Other cultural influences are accelerating the buildup of this war: the average American's perception that she or he has less leisure time; legislation against certain toxic pesticides, looming water and petroleum shortages, to say nothing of both gas prices and Global Warming. These pressures and a profound shift in consciousness that I believe is taking place, will increase the number of enlistments in this war, as the knowledge of alternatives becomes more widespread.

Each of us, in our small place, longs to reconnect with nature and its blessings. That longing is everything. That desire carries the energy that will bring us to a new place.

My Daughter's Lawn

Although there may be cause for tentative celebration about some of the improvements in the big picture, it still comes down to individual efforts. The choices we make as individuals do add up to cultural change, or stagnation, as the case may be. Embedded, as we are, in a culture that seems in many ways to have gone off the rails, we each continue to contribute to environmental problems even when we know better. The subtle pressure to conform impacts each of us, as I found when I spent a year, with my daughter, in her new house in the central New Jersey countryside. I'd gone there to be company for Jan following the sudden death of her husband from a heart attack, and to give myself some time for writing. The new house sits in the middle of four treeless acres.

Out of deference to her late husband's wishes, all four acres had been devoted to lawn, a decision that I found ecologically repugnant. My repugnance intensified when the new mowing tractor arrived. I watched the tractor lesson, all the while thinking, "You won't catch me on that thing! No possible way!"

The mower epitomized all that I'd been moving against in my latter-day environmental awareness. The grit, the industrial macho of it, the wastefulness of it - all this gas, a non-renewable resource, kicking all this CO_2 into the atmosphere, bringing on global warming - and all this terrible noise. None of it made any sense to me.

However, obeying my self-imposed rule for our cohabitation, I said nothing. I watched Jan drive the monster around the property, slaloming in and out around the dogs' Invisible Fence flags; saw the swath she cut through the brown-eyed Susans that were just beginning to get a foothold, and thought, "OK, baby, if this is how you want to spend your Saturdays, be my guest." My way was clear. I would have nothing to do with this abomination called a *lawn*, and eventually she'd catch on, decide that there are better things to do with her time, and let the lawn go back to meadow.

But it didn't happen that way. Once, twice, maybe, in weak moments, I said I'd help with the mowing - just a little bit. "Just the back part. All the rest is yours. And no way will I back that monster down the so-called 'ramp' (two flimsy aluminum tracks that have to be positioned each time) to get it out of the shed."

The Machine From Hell

The first time, I thought I was driving the machine from hell. "What is a 64 year old woman doing bouncing around on this heaving, roaring inferno of bolts and gears and internal (are you sure?), combustion?," I wondered, "Where is the dignity of the aged?"

But on the second mowing, as I opened the throttle to the max, lurching forward and accelerating full speed ahead, blades down, cutting a swath the size of my dining room table through the chicory and Queen Anne's lace, I suddenly understood the macho attraction to huge motors that make a lot of noise. I felt *powerful,* as I never had before. That a small, vulnerable, basically unprotected human could do so much damage in such a short time was truly amazing. Energized by the rush of it, I sat up as straight as I could, squared my jaw, and drew a bead on the far edge of the property.

That must have been the time I decided to take 'er up the ramp myself, bracing for the probable crashing through the shed wall if I should forget the instructions for stopping. I didn't crash, and after that I thought there was nothing I couldn't do with that tractor. I could turn 'er on a dime, and I learned to swerve up so close to the water meter that I nicked it frequently.

I was hooked. Each time I mowed I promised myself it was the last time. Like an alcoholic swearing off the bottle the morning after, I would remind myself of my ecological purity. In my mind I'd go over all the reasons why mowing is a bad addiction.

How soon we forget. A week would go by, then two, and then three. The Queen Anne's lace would pop up again. And the thistles. And the dock. I'd go skulking off to the shed, like a drunk remembering a hidden bottle, and crank 'er up for another shot of raw Power! Yesss! Powwerrrr!

The Turning Point

What was the turning point? What event pulled me back from this degradation? It must have been the killdeer. We'd watched from the window every day in the spring, hoping to see chicks, as she'd sat on her nest in the driveway. We'd swerved around the nest every time we drove in or out of the garage. We'd put Invisible Fence flags around the nest, to warn unsuspecting guests, and we'd run down to the mailbox, to warn delivery trucks. Incubation seemed to take forever and we wondered if, because of all the disturbances, she'd been off the nest too much.

Then, one gentle June morning while Jan was at work, I watched from the dining room window as one, then two, then three, and finally, a fourth miniature killdeer appeared. Valiantly, the two killdeer parents worked together all afternoon to get the chicks to safety. While they'd evidently thought the driveway to be a perfectly sensible location for their nest, it was quite a different story once the babies were hatched. As soon as the last one was strong enough to travel, the evacuation began. One by one the mother would coax the little ones across the vast expanse of lawn to some predetermined safety island, while the father would employ diversionary tactics around the nest. This "island," existing only in the imagination of the mother killdeer, was nothing. Just a place in the lawn where they all collected. As soon as the last one arrived, the mother would start out again, toward another imaginary "island," coaxing and cajoling.

The process took all day and was still going on when Jan arrived home from work. We watched through the window with the field glasses, counting at each "island," one, two, three four - yup, all four chicks made it. Then off they'd troop again in another exodus. The final destination, it appeared, was a green belt of weeds and multiflora roses between Jan's property and the horse trail beyond it. When they reached the farthest "island" before the green belt, I counted, "One, two three . . . ? Here, you count," I said, handing Jan the field glasses. We counted again and again. There were only three. Sadly, we acknowledged that one of the chicks hadn't made it.

Finally, at dusk, we watched the mother and the three remaining chicks disappear one by one into the green belt at the property's edge. That was the last of any killdeer we were to see for months.

It had been a dramatic day, and it still clung to my memory in mid-August, as I zoomed across the front and side of the property on the tractor, like a crazed cowboy. Suddenly, about halfway between the green belt and the driveway, Mrs. Killdeer appeared, running toward me on the ground. I swerved the tractor to avoid her, turned, and gunned toward the other end of the property. On the way back for another pass, there she was again, running toward me. I swerved again, and watched as she patrolled back and forth, never leaving the ground. On the third pass, instead of swerving, I put the tractor in neutral, and just sat there.

The killdeer held her ground, standing about three yards in front of the tractor. An image flashed before my eyes of the student in Tiananmen Square, standing in front of the tank. Mrs. Killdeer lowered her head and stepped toward the tractor. I put it in reverse and slowly backed away. She kept walking toward the tractor. Finally,

I said, "OK, tell me what you want me to do." She began to walk around in an area I hadn't yet mowed. I watched as she circumscribed an area maybe twenty feet in diameter. I put the tractor in gear and slowly went around the area she showed me. An island. And now, and island with weeds so tall that its safety was not imaginary.

That night at dinner, I told Jan about the brave killdeer, facing down the lawn tractor. "I'm not going to mow there anymore", I said simply. "In fact, I'm not going to mow anywhere, unless I can do it the way I want."

Surprisingly, Jan agreed that I could do it any way I wanted to. But I didn't believe her. The next time I mowed, about three weeks later, I tested her sincerity. I mowed around a long dogleg, about five feet wide, right into the middle of the back yard, where, in the springtime, there's a natural watercourse. When I came to a corner of the property, instead of mowing into the corner, I mowed out from it. Another dogleg appeared leading out to where the water meter sticks up, and one along the Invisible Fence lines so we wouldn't have to slalom the flags. I continued to mow around the killdeer safety island, which by now boasted some very mature weeds.

I've never seen the killdeer in that place again, though I still respect her boundaries. Was her performance, that day with the tractor, advanced planning? Was she preparing for next spring's exodus across the lawn? Was she saying, "Next spring, all four will make it!"? I waited for Jan's reaction to my creative mowing. To my surprise, she didn't complain. Knowing that Jan likes butterflies, I began talking about how the thistle attracts them, and about how the dear critters of the field will now have little migration corridors across the lawn. I knew Jan's love of animals would serve me well in this anticipated argument.

The argument never happened. Each time I mowed, I tested more, adding another couple of feet of width to this dogleg, extending that one a bit, starting a new island in the middle of a large expanse of lawn. Each time, Jan said nothing.

Having spoken for butterflies, I started to notice them more myself, swerving to miss them when I encountered them in the path of my mowing, apologizing to them for all the butterflies I'd helped my brother chloroform when I was ten, allowing them to dictate to me which areas to leave natural, as the killdeer had done. Still, no complaints from Jan.

The big test came when the in-laws came up from Florida for a week. I imagined that Jan would be embarrassed by such an unconventional and, by this time, unkempt-looking lawn. I fortified myself with terms like "natural habitat" and "endangered species," preparing for an elaborate explanation. That, too, never occurred.

Lawn Sculpting

Emboldened, I began cutting mower-sized paths through the doglegs and into the green belts, out to the compost heaps and over to the neighbor's property, for easy walking access. I started sculpting elegant curves around the wild areas. Islands that were circles became boring, reminding me of crop circles in reverse. I tried kidneys and "S" shapes and hearts. Gradually the weeds filled in the unmowed areas so that they no longer looked like mistakes. Lovely white, yellow and blue wildflowers bobbled in the breeze. Thistle and clover and Queen Anne's lace, chicory and daisies, brown-eyed Susans and tickseed sunflowers supplied us with continuous cuttings for the dinner table. We no longer called them weeds. The property looked softer; friendlier, I thought, and far more interesting than before. The dogs thought so too, and they began staying outside longer, exploring.

I started to take genuine delight in my art project, quite beyond the mere power rush of driving the tractor. I was in recovery. I was learning to mow in moderation, and my ecological virtue returned. I could mow and still feel like I was doing something for the environment, a compromise to be sure, but "not a bad one, not bad at all," I thought. I was undaunted when the tractor's tire went flat, pumping it up myself, and when the tractor fell off the ramp, crunching sickeningly into the shed door. I started to plan for mowing days with eager anticipation. Now I spent long moments gazing from upstairs windows, sculpting mentally: let's see - that one needs a deeper curve, and a new path over there, yes, a new path - and I could hardly wait for mowing day. Now mowing was, I confess, one of the Great Pleasures in my life.

Did I dare to hope that my unconventional mowing patterns would be honored when I returned to Michigan? Did Mrs. Killdeer dare to hope? Well, yes, I did. I hoped to visit the following spring to see if the killdeer nest would be repeated in the driveway. I hoped to stand in the dining room window with the field glasses and not see *any* chicks, as they made their way safely hidden from human view, across the lawn via the most recently created dogleg, toward the safety island their mother had so gallantly created for them.

It was worth the power withdrawal I suffered when I returned to my postage stamp-sized lawn in Michigan. I plugged in my little Black and Decker electric mower and listened to its modest hum, no louder than a blender. I walked humbly behind it, dragging its nicked, orange umbilical cord. As I did so, I could imagine actual nostalgia for Jan's gas-guzzling, lurching, belching roaring lawn-monster. I knew I'd fondly remember a fine summer of creative lawn sculpting, and a certain fearless killdeer, who faced down a tank in New Jersey's Tiananmen Square.

The Pressure to Conform

And that's how it goes when nature and culture meet, only nature doesn't usually come out the winner, as it did that time. And did nature really win that one? Even with all the killdeer taught me, I'd continued to ride the mowing tractor, mowing right over killdeer eggs, for all I knew.

Although I've moved from the postage stamp yard and now have my own natural habitat yard, I still mow parts of it - paths and clearings and some of the parts the neighbors can see. Why do I mow at all, feeling the way I do? Part of the answer is that I like the contrast of wild and tame, brush and clearing. Animals as well as humans use my paths. I know because I see their tracks and scat there, so I can convince myself that paths are good. But a great deal of my mowing still comes from a wish to conform, and out of a wish not to have my homeowner's insurance cancelled, as I've been told sometimes happens to people who leave their lawns unmowed. Recently I've seen some yards, even in urban settings, where the ecologically devoted owners have torn up the lawn and put in all natives, front and back. While I admire their chutzpah, I know myself well enough to proceed cautiously, shrinking the lawn gradually, hoping the neighbors will get used to it and not be offended by it. I do not handle confrontation well. I get flustered, forget the well-rehearsed rationale and make matters worse. My approach is more conciliatory. I hope to win people over, not alienate them.

The pressure to do things the way everyone else does them is subtle but powerful, perhaps the moreso if unacknowledged. So far I've received no complaints about my wild lawn, though a kindly neighbor offered to mow it for me. I'm lucky to have found a place that's rural enough so that the pressure to conform isn't nearly what it was in the cheek-by-jowl subdivision I lived in before I moved here. But living in the country is no guarantee, as my friends, Robin and Greg, who live in an area that's even more rural than mine, found when they tried to grow a wildflower meadow near their house. On the complaint of a neighbor, they were cited by their township for not mowing their "noxious weeds." The pressure to conform is sometimes not so subtle. This kind of pressure will diminish, I believe, as antiquated weed laws are changed and more and more people wake up to the emerging ecological paradigm.

CHAPTER 3:

Whose Habitat?

. . . as night crept over the heath,
the lone song of the heath bird
would testify to the seriousness
of the land and to its glory.

Jens Jensen, *Siftings*

After that year of lawn-sculpting in New Jersey, I knew my small suburban yard could not accommodate the desire that was growing in my heart. I devoted the next six months to driving up and down country roads, looking for *For Sale* signs. I finally found what I was looking for – an acre and a half that had been grandfathered in when this rural township's master plan was revised to require a minimum 2.5 acres per parcel throughout most of the township. My parcel holds a small house with a fireplace, a pond, and a partly wooded fragment of a forest type where oak and hickory trees dominate, known as an *oak-hickory barrens*.

When I moved here, the entire acre and a half was mowed to its edges. My first act was to mow a small open area near the deck and a path around the pond, leaving the rest unmowed. Next, I mowed a small area at the west end of the pond where I established a wooden bench for pond meditation. The last open area in the back to be mowed was a small clearing in the woods, east of the pond, where I dug a fire pit. Tree stumps were dragged from behind the pole barn and placed in a circle around the fire pit. I call this clearing "Stump-henge." These open areas, connected by mowed paths, would be the only back yard areas that would be mowed; all the rest would be left alone to grow wild.

The main activity that first summer was pulling down the farm fencing that surrounded the property and isolated it from the wet prairie to the west and the woods to the east. I announced to all the animals within hearing distance that the welcome mat was out; this was to be a sanctuary where they would not be hassled or hunted down. This would be habitat they could count on.

Although my son Jeff, who pulled down most of the fence, might not have thought so, these activities were small. I hadn't the slightest idea of what I was doing, but believed that by being attentive to the natural world as this place expresses it, I could learn slowly what might be required of me to make it attractive to the wild animals that still inhabit this sub-rural landscape (now called a "development hot spot"). At the time, I had only the fuzziest idea about native plants. I suppose I'd heard about them. I suppose I didn't think they were important. As it turns out, the chief requirement for creating wildlife habitat, (or so I thought), and the hardest one, was to do nothing.

A Pot of Gold

Five years later, looking out my studio window, this is what I saw: Eight deer appeared by the pond, near the bench. Six of them were adolescents, their coats tawnier in color, with just a hint of dapple, their demeanor friskier than that of the two older deer. Slowly, the eight deer worked their way toward the house, perhaps attracted there by the activity around the bird feeders or the hostas growing there. One young deer was full of vinegar, jumping sideways, jostling the older deer, undoing their dignity. This yearling suddenly bolted and took off at lightning speed around the pond. By the time he'd completed the circuit and started around for the second time, the other five young deer had joined the chase, leaping and lunging around and around the pond with carefree abandon while the two adult deer looked on indulgently. For a quarter of an hour, maybe more, I sat transfixed in my studio window as this astonishing performance continued. *Around and around and around* they went. Occasionally the six yearlings disappeared into the woods for a few seconds, only to come bounding back to resume their breathtaking, exuberant chase. Finally exhausted, I supposed, all eight deer disappeared slowly into the woods, and the show was over.

Earlier that day I'd absent-mindedly doodled a pot of gold at the end of the rainbow. I'd puzzled over what, if anything, it might mean. Now, sitting at my window, I knew. I drew a deep breath of gratitude, understanding that I had just been given a Great Gift. This, I knew, was the pot of gold! That my hard work, (or my decision not to work), that my heart's fervent desire should be answered so abundantly, with such joy, such grace, such beauty, was stunning testimony to the responsiveness of the natural world.

What I saw that day would probably never have happened on an ordinary lawn. I knew my back yard had become a place safe enough for deer to play. It was an undeniable affirmation of what I'd only weakly intuited five years before - that beneath our carefully tended lawns and patios, our macadam roads and black-topped parking lots, there is *Something Else*, shimmering with radiance, waiting to be released; *Something Else*, vibrant and eager to emerge. This radiance becomes available whenever we get out of its way. It rewards our heart's desire in unexpected ways; it responds to our deepest yearnings. Now I know this is true, although when I set out to create "wildlife habitat," I only half believed it. It had seemed a small decision, not to mow, yet the desire behind it was huge. It was a desire to do something for the natural world upon which we humans have so imposed our will; to get out of its way, to listen to what it wants.

Listening to nature is nothing new. The transcendentalists so prominent in our history have all urged it. But never before have we had such an imperative to do so. The fact that we have to make a conscious decision to sharpen our awareness of the natural world, into which we are inextricably woven, is testimony to how far away from it our hearts have strayed.

There are powerful forces telling us not to listen; to do it our way; to dominate the landscapes we think we own. Counteracting those forces, two important initiatives are converging: Backyard Wildlife Habitat and the cultivation of native plants.

Backyard Wildlife Habitat

Only recently has it begun to be recognized that although humans may hold "title" to the land, it belongs to other species as well. I became acutely aware of this one day about 35 years ago, when I was riding the family horse, Danny Boy, through the fields behind our house.

Just three days before, I'd ridden to a place near the woods where both sides of the path were covered as far as the eye could see with dense lupine blossoms. As I'd walked Danny Boy slowly down the path, the intense blue of the lupines had permeated the area and I'd slipped ecstatically into it, feeling that Danny Boy was enveloped in blue as I was. A hawk circled gracefully overhead. The hawk, too, participated in the blue ecstasy, of that I'd been sure.

Now, three days later, Danny Boy seemed drawn again to the same spot, as I was. It took no reining to steer him there. It was where he wanted to go. But as we followed the curve of the path toward the woods, Danny Boy stopped in his tracks, startled by what lay ahead. Bulldozers had flattened the entire area. Raw earth now lay, bleeding, it seemed, at our feet. The lupines were gone. The trees beyond the lupines were gone. The hawk circled overhead as he had done before, but now with anguished cries of grief and despair.

Though I did not hold title to this land, it belonged to my heart. Though the hawk did not hold title to it, it was his hunting ground. It had been taken rudely away in two short days, without permission from the hawk, the horse, the lupines, the Karner Blue butterflies who depended on the lupines, or the human.

Hawks, deer and foxes, elk and wolves, skunks, opossum, and raccoons – and many species whose names we don't even know - are increasingly being pushed out of their habitats by human settlements and development. Some of them have adapted well to suburban living, but the humans they interact with have not adapted as well to them, and they are often viewed as pests and menaces. Just ask anyone who has had a family of raccoons rearranging the furniture in the attic, or lost a corn crop or tulips to deer. The hunting ground or war theatre has shifted from their territory to our territory.

In much the same way, the unlanded people of Old Europe were pushed off of land they'd previously been free to forage and farm. The time of the enclosure, when feudal lords all over Europe simply fenced in the land they wanted for themselves, is remembered as a terrible crisis for the common people, who had been free to hunt, grow and gather their own food and fuel up until then. Those people who did remain on the land became serfs, working primarily to produce food for their masters, with only a small percentage of it allowed for them.

Settlers of the North American continent created a similar crisis for the American Indians, pushing them off the land that had been theirs for centuries, isolating them on barren reservations where they could barely eke out a living. In much the same way, we're marginalizing animals that formerly had large areas in which to make their living.

When I complained at my local township hall about a new development that was about to manifest in the area where I live, I was told patronizingly not to worry about "the little deers. They can move somewhere else," I was assured. "Where?" I asked in despair, knowing how drastically their territories are shrinking. One of the answers to that question is that deer and other wild animals are increasingly showing up in peoples' yards (where else can they go?), where they are increasingly unwelcome.

Unwelcome Visitors

While an alarming number of species are facing extinction, the same cannot be said of the raccoon, squirrel, skunk, rabbit, mole, and deer populations who have developed a taste for suburban living. In North America there are more white-tailed deer now, for example, than there used to be. Thanks to a combination of modern agriculture, the elimination of predators, and urban sprawl, the U.S. white-tail deer population has actually *increased* from less than half a million at the turn of the century to an estimated 20 million now.[20] Without the natural predators that formerly kept their population in check, their numbers have multiplied as their territories have shrunk. Seeking new food sources, they wind up in peoples' yards, where they are likely to find nature's fast-food delicacies. They also feast on some of the rapidly disappearing native flora in undeveloped areas, posing a conundrum for ecologists. If the deer populations in these habitats were in good balance this wouldn't happen. More on this later.

Not everyone welcomes the deer as I do. My affection for them, like others' was tempered the year they wiped out my hosta bed. Being friends doesn't mean you have to let them eat you out of house and home, and I'm looking for ways to dampen the deer's enthusiasm for hostas. Trouble is, I've put out more than a welcome mat for them. I've laid out a veritable banquet in their honor, it seems to them. And at a time when their habitat is decreasing exponentially, where else can they go?

Deer are not the only ones. If you really want some fun, try raccoons in the attic, as my friend Luellen did. It ended up costing her weeks of sleepless nights and hundreds of dollars to have them carted off. For those who don't want such a close association with the wild, or maybe just want to keep furry friends out of the house, the tulips, the lilies, the hostas and the corn, repellents do help, as does an aggressively barking dog or an electric fence.

Certain native plants can help to keep wildlife out of areas where you don't want them. Canada geese, who love to graze on mowed turfgrass, don't like tall grass and will avoid your pond and lake edges if native grasses are encouraged to grow there. The geese, who are concerned about predators hiding in the bulrushes, will seek more open access to waterfront.

Just keeping your mower five or ten feet away from the water's edge will successfully deter most geese. Lakeside property owners who have left such a buffer-strip have found they are no longer bothered by goose-droppings. The accelerated eutrophication caused by goose droppings along the water's edge is also diminished. Some lakefront property associations that have employed this technique have found they no longer need to organize goose-roundups to relocate the geese. This practice, which is questionable from a humanitarian point of view is, in any case, largely ineffective in the long run, because the geese keep returning to the same places where lawns are mowed up to the water's edge. They return because lawns at water's edge are ideal habitat for Canada geese.

Deer and other four-leggeds (sometimes) find scented geraniums repugnant and will avoid an area surrounded by them. Deer especially eschew pungent herbs, such as rosemary, fennel, and rue.

"Seventy percent of urban wildlife problems can be eliminated if food and lodging opportunities are removed,"[21] says Al, our local animal control guy. Luellen's raccoons must have been part of the other 30%.

Those of us who provide food and lodging for wildlife have already blurred the line between them and us humans. That blurry line is sometimes a fine one between providing wildlife habitat and allowing the wildlife to invade *your* habitat. How are they supposed to know that it's OK to make a nest in the yard but not in the house? "Raccoons rabble-rouse in your chimney because you cut down the old hollow oak and a chimney will substitute fine,"[22] opines nature writer Jonathan Schechter.

I read about a woman who had no screens on her windows so the birds could fly in and out, which they did with some abandon. (She encouraged them with sunflower seeds.) Charmed by the idea, I was ready to try it myself, until I thought about the mosquitoes and the bird-droppings, to say nothing of the mice, squirrels, and raccoons that might also opt for the great indoors, given the opportunity. That helped me draw a line between my habitat and theirs. Peaceful co-existence is more to my liking.

When humans are clear about their boundaries, human/wildlife co-habitation is usually peaceful. In the summertime a family of raccoons and a family of skunks come every night to feast on the sunflower seeds that have escaped from my bird feeders. The skunks are trustworthy as long as they don't feel threatened. The raccoons, on the other hand, have been bold and sassy, destroying several bird feeders before they trained me to bring the feeders in at night. The catch 22 in this scenario is that bringing the feeders inside invites the mice inside. So now I'm thinking of only feeding the birds in midwinter, when the raccoons are hibernating. In the long view, encouraging the birds' dependence on our largesse probably doesn't help them much either. Better to plant the things they evolved with, native seed and nectar-bearing forbs (herbaceous, non-woody plants other than grass, usually called wildflowers), grasses, and berry-bearing bushes.

My most recent challenge is moles. They like the little bit of lawn I do have for their tunnels. Never bothered much by weeds, I've been content with a "Fifty mile-an-hour-lawn." (Driving by at fifty miles an hour, you don't notice the weeds and it doesn't look so bad). Weeds at least are green. But moles kill even the weeds, leaving the lawn ugly and scarred. Now it's an "Eighty mile-an-hour lawn."

At first I thought if I ignored the moles they'd lose interest, like obnoxious children. But the moles have taken advantage of my laissez faire approach. Our relationship is rapidly deteriorating to a point beyond rapprochement.

Now, mowing the corrugated expanse formerly known as "lawn" is an exercise in futility because there's nothing to mow. The mower lurches from hill to hill, - one wheel wobbling loosely, threatening to come off. Plopping down at the top of a molehill, into which it sinks, the mower growls, and spits out a cascade of dirt caught by the blade.

I've ordered milky spore, which, once it gets established, is supposed to discourage moles by discouraging the grubs they love.

(Since ordering it, I've read that its benefits in Michigan, where I live, are limited.) And I've circled the battery-powered sonic mole-repeller in the gardening catalog. But I'd rather just talk to the moles. Couldn't I convince them that I mean them no harm if they'd just leave my little bit of lawn alone?

My friend Deanne thinks the moles are speaking to me, if I would only listen. What are the moles telling me? Maybe they're saying I don't need to mow at all; that I don't need *any* lawn. My plan had been to gradually shrink the lawn by expanding the native beds, but maybe the moles are telling me not to be so gradual. If all of it were tall natives, no one would see their tunnels. Hence, a "Ten mile-an-hour lawn".

The moles and the deer, as well as many other wild animals, are adapting to our inviting landscapes where well-watered, fertilized shrubs provide them with easy handouts, and in some neighborhoods, they live year-round in dangerously close proximity to humans for this reason. Even coyotes are finding hospitality in some suburbs, which provide them with rodents, deer meat, an occasional housecat, and geese, who, because of their near domestication, have lost their wariness.

In native habitats that are in healthy balance, the deer and coyote populations are kept within natural limits. When these habitats are given over to housing developments, the deer and the coyotes have no place else to look for food. The rich easy diet they find in our yards encourages their reproduction. We declare war on the deer, and on the opossums, the squirrels, and the raccoons, who are attracted to our bird feeders. It's a strange crisis for the animals, caught between a wealth of unnatural food sources and few places to call their own.

The crisis of the animals is our crisis. We might remind ourselves that the Word, "Animal" is derived from the Greek word, "animus", which means soul. If we do not make a place in our hearts for the animals of the world we will surely lose our soul. They bring us a radical aliveness that is missing in our increasingly urbanized world. That goes for insects too, many of which are beneficial in a variety of ways, including pollination. It goes as well for the native grasses, sedges, forbs, shrubs and trees in which they make their home.

The species we see in our yards and at our bird feeders are only a small percentage of the variety that used to be here. The 2000 EAD Bulletin notes, "When the Endangered Species Act was enacted in 1973, only 109 species in the United States were recognized as imperiled. Today, more than 10 times that number is recognized as threatened or endangered. Scientists estimate that the global rate of extinctions has accelerated to between 100 and 10,000 times their natural pace set by nature and evolution."[23] In an article in the National Wildlife Federation's Spring, 2000 *Habitats*, Jeff Flocke observed, "About one-third of the 200,000 plant and animal species in the United States are threatened or endangered. Of the 1,100 native plants inventoried on Staten Island in the 1700's, 430 are now extinct.[24]

Perhaps even more alarming is the finding of *the World Conservation Union*, which states that in the U.S., 29% of the plants (the foundation of the food chain) are at risk of extinction.[25] When they go, the insects, birds and other animals associated with them go as well. Those beings who evolved with those native plants will lose their food-sources and homes. Remnant survivors, if there are any, often lack the genetic variability for the continuance of the species. With wild places being replaced by 50 million lawns across America, *the National Wildlife Foundation* notes that the world is facing an endangered species crisis the like of which has not been seen since the extinction of the dinosaurs.

PART II:

Natives

CHAPTER 4:

Where the Wild Things are

The real worth of the landscaper lies in his ability to give to humanity the blessing of nature's spiritual values as they are interpreted in his art. The field is boundless, and there is no need of importing from foreign shores.

Jens Jensen, *Siftings*

A Crisis and an Opportunity

To many Americans, the *lawn* represents the last stronghold of individual decision-making power. Surprisingly, this can be good news. The same situation (individual land ownership) that has led to lawn hegemony can now be used to begin to undo that hegemony. I can plant natives where my lawn used to be. If I choose not to have a lawn, should that not be my right as a landowner? Well, as it turns out, it's not that simple. Many property owners who have tried to create wildlife habitat instead of lawn have run into local ordinances that prohibit or severely limit them from doing so. This too is changing, as we will see in Chapter 17. As more and more people transform their lawns into wildlife habitat, the iron grip of lawn hegemony is gradually being loosened.

A Noble Savage?

When I started my backyard wildlife habitat I didn't have any clear picture in my mind of what that might be. Inspired by Sara Stein's book, *Noah's Garden*, I had a vague idea that I wanted my property to be natural and welcoming to wildlife. I wanted to be a noble savage. While I was devoted to the notion of learning whatever this small piece of land could teach me, I refused to become a botanist. I didn't want to know the names of things. I wanted the land, not the books, to teach me.

Backyard Wildlife Habitat

Then I heard about *The National Wildlife Federation*, which certifies individual properties and schoolyards as "Backyard Wildlife Habitats." In early 2000, over 1,000 backyard wildlife habitats had been certified. Eight years later, that number had increased nearly 100-fold, to 97,429.

Only four elements are needed: food, water, cover, and places to raise young. No place is too small. A seven by seven foot area with a birdbath, a birdhouse, a birdfeeder and a tree is enough. I discovered that my property, without my even trying very hard, already had all of the elements needed for certification.

I filled out the application form, drew a map of my property, and took some pictures to send with my application. They took my word for it. Nobody came to check up on me. Investigators were not sent out to discern whether or not I had the right kind of berry bushes. Since then, the Wildlife Federation has trained cadres of local certifiers. If I were applying for certification today, a local certifier would probably show up to verify that the right things are here.

A few weeks after I sent in my application, a nice certificate arrived in the mail, and a small weatherproof sign to put out by the road. Shortly after that, a reporter came out, took pictures and interviewed me for the local newspaper. When the story was published I met Trish, a neighbor who shared my interest. That was the beginning of an enriching and rewarding friendship.

Trish is an Advanced Master Gardener, deeply involved in the world of wildflowers, perennials, hardy plants, and more recently, native plants. She knows the names of things. We've gone to workshops together. We've both joined the local chapter of *Wild Ones*, a national organization devoted to promoting native plants and natural landscaping (see *Resources, Appendix A).

Trish and I have shared our knowledge, our failures, and our colds. We've egged each other on. With help from volunteers and encouragement from *The National Wildlife Federation*, Trish developed a backyard wildlife habitat at her kids' school. Her ravenous hunger for knowledge about plants and ecology astonishes me. It was through Trish that I began to realize that wildlife habitat and native plants go together like a horse and carriage.

Now I want to know the names of things. And I'm beginning to grasp that it's not enough just to know their *common* names. It's better if you know their *Latin* names as well, since common names change from region to region while Latin ones do not. I'm still not a botanist, or even an aspiring one. But it's yet another case of *the more you know the more you know you don't know*. Underneath every new thing I learn is a universe of more to learn. I've only just begun to get a handle on the lingo: Natives, exotics, forbs, prairies, fens. And I ask myself, "*Out of what latent grandiosity do I find myself writing about this in a book?*"

A Sense of Place

With the native landscapes that are showing up across the country, a new awareness of one's bioregional place is becoming evident. Traveling across the country, there's new delight in experiencing the flora unique to each region. Even now, in most places, a landscape in Baltimore is indistinguishable from a landscape in South Carolina. Daryl Morrison, one of the many gurus of the native landscape movement, speaks of his *topofilia*, or love of many different places, and the joy he experiences with the variety of distinctive native landscapes he encounters in his travels. He describes a *Eureka!* feeling that says, "I know where I am!"

Anyone hoping to deepen their *sense of place* would do well to live in the company of native plants that have evolved there over thousands of years. Robert Grese, a passionate advocate of native landscapes, says that natives express the essence of the unique region where they are found. That *essence* consists of more than just the plants. It implies as well their natural associates, the climate and the soil. Extending that even further, it may be noted that natural landscapes tend to take on the character of their caretakers. Each of the natural landscapes I've seen hereabouts has a uniqueness that, even within the same bioregion, reflects the character of the property owner; a uniqueness seldom found in traditional landscapes.

In his book, *The Wooing of Earth*, Rene' Dubos speaks of the difference between an *environment* and a *place*. The catalyst for the conversion of an *environment* to a *place*, he says, is the deep experience of an area, not as a thing, but as a living organism. He refers to a fitness that is achieved, "only after slow progressive reciprocal adaptations and therefore requires a certain stability of relationships between persons, societies, and places."[26]   The same can be said of the plants native to a "place".

CHAPTER 5:

Native Plants

In a survey of property owners in Southeast Michigan, 30% of respondents believed they have native plants on their property. Chances are, most of the plants they thought were "natives" are not natives at all, but the chicory and Queen Anne's lace that dotted the open fields many of us knew as children. It was with some surprise that I learned the ancestors of these "wild flowers" are not native to the North American continent, but were brought here by European settlers.

Most people define a native plant as any plant whose forebears were growing on the North American continent *before* European settlement. Narrowing the definition further, a plant cannot truly be said to be native to a particular *bioregion* unless it evolved there.

Many natives are fading from memory almost as fast as they are going extinct. I realized when I read a list of plants native to my region, that though I recognized many of their names - Joe-Pye weed (Eupatorium maculatum), butterfly weed (Asclepias tuberosa), bulrush (Scirpus atrovirens), for example, – I hadn't seen them since I was a child. I wasn't sure I'd recognize them if I did see them. Many others on the list were totally unknown to me. I now believe it is a natural scandal of major proportions that not only are we causing the disappearance of these wonderful species in all their amazing diversity and beauty, but they are being erased from our memories as well. It shouldn't come as a surprise, then, to learn that although most children can easily recognize more than a thousand corporate logos, they can't recognize as many as ten native plants. Think about it. Which is worse:

to be gone, or gone *and forgotten?* When these exquisite life forms are gone even from memory, they will be gone forever from human consciousness - an anthropocentric thought that posits a profound existential question. If we can't even *remember* them, will it be as if they never existed at all?

A critical outcome of this difficulty is the loss of the other species that have evolved with them, and who depend on them for food, nesting, and cover. Although native plants are disappearing at an alarming rate, it's not too late for some. We still have time to reinstate them in our yards, in their ecosystems, and in our memories. Even though it's closing fast, we do have a window of opportunity.

Jens Jensen, a natural landscape pioneer of the late 1800's and early 1900's, observed, "Art must come from within, and the only source from which the art of landscaping can come is our native landscape. It cannot be imported from foreign shores and be our own."[27] As we shall see in Chapter 10, Jensen believed that "Every plant has its fitness and must be placed in its proper surroundings so as to bring out its full beauty."

Local natives, i.e., plants that have evolved for this particular microclimate and bioregion, are better adapted to it than the same species that comes from even another North American bioregion. Generally speaking, a plant does best in the place where it evolved. For its fullest fitness, a plant needs *provenance*, or its "place of origin," and this means more than geography and climate. It means as well, all the other plants and animals and insects that evolved with it in symbiotic relationship. It means the hydrology and the particular soil type, and even the indigenous microbes found in its place of origin.

An exception to this rule is a class of plants known as invasive exotics or alien species which do better away from home because the natural controls that keep them from taking over are missing in their new environs. A plant that is well-behaved in its hometown will often lose its inhibitions in another locale and trash the place. This will be explored in more detail in the next chapter.

Some experts say a native plant, regardless of its species, should have evolved within a 150-mile radius of its present location. Purists would narrow that even further, to a 25 or 30-mile radius, and here's why: While there's much to be said for the benefits of genetic diversity, there is also a danger that by introducing genes from another locale to a local population, its sustainability can be undermined. In the plant-world, there is a fine and often unclear line between healthy cross-pollination and gene pollution. And it is a line that is not well understood.[28]

There's a lot we don't know about how evolution works things out in ecosystems, and the complexities may well lie beyond our comprehension. For this reason, although a nursery may sell plants that are native to the North American continent, the chances of their being local genotypes, well adapted to local climate and soil conditions, are slim. Horticultural varieties, and plants that have been bred for certain characteristics (cultivars), even though they may be natives, should be avoided. Bill Schneider, our local native plant guru, recommends a conservative approach of seeking out local genotypes, even though they may be hard to find. Currently, most regions do have one or two nurseries that specialize in local genotypes, and some of them are beginning to supply other local nurseries. But it's still a "buyer beware" situation.

Native Grasses and Sedges

A native plant can be a tree, a shrub, a fern, a forb (usually called a wildflower), a sedge, or a grass. Native grasses, sedges, and rushes are often-overlooked important elements in a native landscape. They offer texture and variety to any landscape, and they help hold up taller forbs.

In most ecosystems, it's the grasses that knit things together. Native grasses go deeper than our turfgrass lawns, literally and figuratively. Some native big bluestem (grass) roots go as deep as 15 - 20 feet. Their depth is lateral as well, for their health includes all the other grasses around them, all the wildflowers and trees in association with them, and all of the animals and insects that dwell there and whose lives are intertwined with theirs.

Because ornamental grasses have already found wide acceptance, I believe the native grasses are not far behind. Warm-season native grasses, such as big and little bluestem, (Andropogons gerardii and scoparius), indiangrass, (Sorghastrum nutans), and bottlebrush grass, (Hystrix patula), have an architectural beauty that makes them attractive for home landscapes. Their shimmering seed heads and remarkable colors, ranging from deep bronze through purple to gold, add interest to autumn and winter landscapes. These warm-season grasses offer food and nesting cover for wildlife, and knit together the native forbs that are gradually replacing traditional perennials in many home landscapes. The cool-season native grasses, which present their seeds earlier in the summer, complement these riches. A combination of the two can provide a continuous food source for seed-loving wildlife.

Perhaps lesser known is the hydrological service these grasses provide. Their remarkable root systems, as well as those of other prairie plants, penetrate deep into the soil, absorbing storm water runoff in impressive amounts. Some of these grasses are called "clay-busters" for their soil reconditioning attributes. Many municipalities are beginning to incorporate native grasses and rushes in ditches and swales for storm water management. For both cost-saving and effectiveness, these native plantings have been shown to far outperform traditional pipe and retention systems.

Some enthusiasts are replacing their turfgrass lawns with native grasses. Grasses that can substitute for turfgrass:

Buffalograss (Buchleo dactyloides), is a favorite in many parts of the country. It grows to a height of only 4 to 6 inches. Increasingly used for golf courses and athletic fields, this drought-resistant, warm-season grass offers a smooth appearance even when left unmowed.

Pennsylvania sedge (Carex pensylvanica), though not technically a grass, is a creeping foliage that has a grassy look. Widely distributed throughout the eastern and central U.S., it grows up to 6 to 8 inches when left unmowed. In oak-hickory ecosystems such as the one where I live, Pennsylvania sedge is a "matrix" species, acting as the "glue" that holds the system together.

The slow-growing Red Fescue (Festuca rubra), is another favorite in many locales. It grows to only 8 to 12 inches. It does well in shade and drought and can withstand both the cold of northern climates and the heat of the upper South. It thrives in dry, infertile soil.

Junegrass, (Koeleria macranta), a grass that grows in bunches, does well in sandy, infertile, droughty soil. Little Bluestem (Schizachryium scoparium), the native-grass darling of the Midwest, is a warm-season grass whose attractive plumes grow about 2 - 3 feet tall. In winter, the rusty-orangeish color of the small stand of little blue stem that hugs my front walkway gives a graceful color contrast against the blue-shadowed snow that piles up behind it.

While some native grasses may be found growing alone in large patches, in the wild they are most often found mixed in with other native plants - forbs, shrubs and trees. Their greatest vigor and usefulness is to be found as part of a diverse ecosystem. A lawn made up of a single native grass, like a buffalograss lawn, is certainly preferable to turfgrass. But it should be remembered that to use a native grass in this way, as a monoculture, is to take it out of its context. Its best place is as part of a diverse ecosystem.

Benefits of Native Plants

Native plant communities provide beneficial natural functions that conventional lawns do not. "They do not require irrigation; they need no or infrequent mowing; lawn maintenance services are not needed."[29] They reduce storm water runoff and soil erosion. They prevent siltation in streams. Many native plants improve water quality by taking up pollutants in contaminated groundwater. They protect water quality by avoiding the need for fertilizers and pesticides. They contribute to peace and quiet by eliminating or reducing the need for noisy lawn mowers, which also reduces the amount of smog and CO_2 going into the atmosphere. They save money and labor.

Native plants have evolved specific characteristics that have adapted them exceedingly well to a particular place. Native plant populations often have disease resistances that are missing in many garden plants. Their root systems reach down deep into the soil where moisture remains even during dry spells. Normal rainfall, even when punctuated with prolonged dry spells, is sufficient for natives.

Native landscapes get nutrients from deep down, and know how to make the most of them. They need no fertilizer and in fact do better without it. Because they aren't bred for uniformity, they're capable of coming up with diverse adaptations. They preserve genetic integrity.

The elaborate root systems of native plants mean they help to keep moisture in the soil and in the aquifers. By breaking up hard soil and clay, they increase the soil's ability to capture, cleanse, and absorb water, aiding in the groundwater recharge process. Instead of running off the hard-packed sod of turfgrass, carrying pesticides and fertilizers, flooding storm sewers, silting rivers and eroding hillsides, the rainwater is simply absorbed into the soil where it falls. This miracle of hydrology is not easy to comprehend, but it works so powerfully that many industrial parks are now incorporating native plantings into their landscapes as a way of countering the deleterious effects of storm water runoff.

Native plants are essential components in their ecosystems, providing food for beneficial insects and animals. They occupy vital niches in the web of life. Without them the web begins to collapse.

Individual natives are part of a system requiring certain other natives nearby for their vitality. Native plant grower Bill Schneider emphasizes the importance of considering the whole area and not just the individual plants. When you're planting natives, you're planting *a system*, a *community*, he insists, and each plant relies on other plants in the system for its fullest vigor. Schneider also insists that every microregion on your property has unique characteristics requiring different combinations of natives to reach its fullest potential.

CHAPTER 6:

Planning, Planting, Maintaining

I don't bust sod. That's my rule. If I have to bust sod to do it, it isn't worth doing. Instead, in the fall, I haul a bucket of water and some newspapers to the place where, with my garden hose, I've outlined a new bed on the lawn. Sitting there on my milk-crate, I serenely dip four newspaper pages together in the water then spread them out on the lawn, within the outlined area. The wetness keeps the newspapers from blowing away. I keep doing this untill the new bed area is covered with newspapers. Then I get muscular, wheeling mulch from the mulch pile and dumping it on top of the newspapers until they're covered with 2-3 inches of mulch. A little raking to distribute the mulch and that's it!

Well, almost. Now all I have to do is wait until spring, while the newspapers kill off the turfgrass and the worms and the microbes are busy intermingling mulch and newspapers and soil. When spring comes, *voila!* There's a beautiful friable bed just waiting to be planted. Of course, I've spent the winter refining the drawing of the bed that I've taped to my kitchen wall, so that by spring, I have a pretty good idea of what goes where, and how many of what native plants I'll need.

After a couple of trips to local native plant growers and maybe a native plant sale or two, it's just a matter of sticking them in the ground. For that part, I usually fill up each hole with water before putting in the root-ball, just to give them a good start. If it doesn't rain, I keep everything moist for about a month. After that, depending on the weather, I only water every few days, then once a week, then only in a dry spell. Except for pulling the occasional weed that shows up that's pretty much it for the first summer, while the roots are getting established.

Contrary to common belief, native landscapes are not totally self-maintaining. As with so many things in my life, I learned this the hard way. While it is true that they can survive most droughts and are virtually free from harmful insects and immune to most plant pathogens, native landscapes still need tending. The most notable problem is weeds. Even in a well-established native landscape, weeds will show up wherever there's an opening. Weeds have evolved to do this and they do it very well, often masquerading as benign plants so convincingly that it takes a discerning eye to tell the difference. Also, some *natives* can be pretty aggressive. Keeping them in their place can take some tending.

Some bold (and in my eyes, heroic) pioneers are putting native prairies or meadows where their front lawns used to be. When an existing lawn or non-native planting is replaced with exclusively native plant communities, it's usually called "restoration." This implies that something was there to restore. More frequently, there isn't. *Revegetation* might be a better word to use for this kind of project. Besides taking out the existing lawn, a purist restoration, or revegetation project would probably involve the elimination of all perennial trees, shrubs, and flowers that are not native to the region.

Revegetation or restoration projects, like replacing a lawn with a wildflower meadow or a native prairie, are important because they go beyond the mere preservation of natives. They help eliminate alien species as well. Kudos to those hardy souls who go so far.

If you want to replace your lawn with a meadow or a prairie, your first step would be would be to kill the existing grass and weeds. There are several ways to do this. Some recommend using a *-cide* for this job. Some herbicides are said to be less toxic to humans and are believed to cause no harm to nearby plants, though I have heard of tree roots being damaged by even the most mild-mannered herbicides. Personally, I wouldn't use any of them, having pledged to keep my use of *-cides* to a minimum. I'd probably have to bust sod if I were to attempt such a project. Maybe in another lifetime.

In case you want to try it, the following information has been gathered from several sources for the benefit of the reader, who will not, hopefully, fly by the seat of the pants as I've done. Here's what you do. With a sod-cutter, the top layer of grass and roots must be stripped off. This leaves a weed-free planting area. If the soil is compacted, rototilling may be in order, but remember that weeds *love* disturbed soil. If you do disturb the soil, you may want to wait till the weeds have appeared, then hoe or cultivate them out just before planting.

You can *sterilize* the soil instead, by covering it with black or clear plastic with mulch on top. This kills off any weed seeds that are in the soil, but it's probably not practical for a large area and you might have qualms about the length of time it takes for plastic to degrade.

The next step is to rake it smooth, then plant the area with seed or plugs. Bill Schneider recommends, depending on conditions, 3 to12 pounds of seed per acre (5 oz/square foot), if you're using Canada Wild Rye you'll need less than half of that. If you're using plugs, it will take one or two plugs every 1-2 square feet, or you can use some of both seed and plugs. Plugs will need 2-3 inch deep holes. It's best to get the advice of a native plant grower, as the amount of seed needed can vary according to the site. I'm not giving you a plant list because natives are bioregion-specific. Your local extension service, if you have one, can tell you who the local native plant growers are in your area.

When planting seeds, rake the seeded area lightly and cover it with a very light layer of soil. This could be rolled with a lawn roller, but it's probably not necessary. The last thing is to strew the area with a light layer of chopped, weed-free straw (not hay). Spray gently, and keep the area moist through the first year except during weeks when it rains.

If you live in the Midwest and plant black-eyed Susans (Rudbeckia hirta), sunflowers, (Helianthus), goldenrods (solidagos) and asters, (Aster novae-angliae, laevis, and macrophyllus), beneficial insects will be attracted to them. These will counteract many of the destructive insects that may be around, making the use of insecticides unnecessary. That's how it works in a naturally balanced environment. You can also encourage these and other beneficial insects by spraying your garden with sugar water or lemon-lime soda.

Native plantings are an exercise in patience for those of us who like instant everything, so be prepared for disappointment in the beginning. It may take a couple of years before your native planting looks like much. A native landscape that's supposed to look like a garden will always need occasional weeding and trimming, although a lot less than a garden of cultivars would. Your native prairie will probably need extra attention for the first couple of years, but once established, it should be virtually self-sustaining except for weeding, and an occasional burn or strategic once-a-year mowing.

The Burn

Did I say *burn*? Did I say *heroic*? If you're restoring a wildflower meadow or a prairie on your property, it will need to be *burned* every two-to-three years. (Some experts disagree about the frequency.) Following the devastating grass fires at Grand Canyon and Bandolier National Park in New Mexico in 2000, the need to have such burns strictly prescribed and supervised is seen as more acute than ever. Even though these burns were prescribed and carefully monitored, they got out of control, causing the heartbreaking loss of buildings. As a result, it may be harder to obtain burn permits in the future.

But the need for periodic burning in natural or restored prairie areas is critical to their health. The plants that grow there have evolved along with the natural disturbance of fire, and many of them require fire to thrive. The fire controls many of the undesirable plants, such as invasive exotics. The native plants, the ones that are adapted to fire, will then spread and benefit from the fire-enriched soil. Because fire warms the ground, your prairie will have a longer growing season.

It's true that the fire will cause some air pollution, but this is minimal and more than offset by carbon gain in the soil and the resulting healthy ecosystem, which will then have a greater capacity to filter particulates and carbon dioxide. Certainly any air pollution that might result from your burn will be far less than if you were mowing the same-size lawn with an internal combustion mower.

You'll need a permit from your local fire department, and they may welcome your "burn" as a training opportunity for their firefighters. Weather conditions such as temperature, wind-direction and strength, humidity and moisture, will all need to be taken into consideration.

If you're burning a large area, you'll want to burn only one part of it at a time, to give wildlife a chance to escape into burrows or surrounding areas. When the burned area recovers in a few weeks, it will be better able to support wildlife than before. If you live in a place where burning is prohibited, a once-a-year mowing of your prairie or meadow can accomplish much of the same benefits as a burn. May and June should be avoided, as ground-nesting birds may be present.

Although I haven't yet tried a burn, many of the things I've done (or not done) on my property are unconventional. Fortunately I live in a place where, with some caution, I can get away with these things (so far). Obviously, you're more likely to run into trouble in suburbs and urban neighborhoods. But in case you think it can't be done, I know of a man who burns his urban front yard prairie every two years. The neighbors love it, celebrating it with a block party.

Seed and Plant Collecting Protocols

Each plant in Bill Schneider's nursery is tagged with a number that tells him exactly when and where the seed or cutting was collected, and exactly what kind of conditions it requires to thrive. In case you're tempted to collect seeds or dig plants from the wild, well, don't. "Collecting plants or seeds in the wild can devastate local plant populations."[30] If you know someone who has natives on their property, and can get their permission, it's OK to gather seeds, but it must be done judiciously, leaving the larger portion of the seeds where they are, to regenerate in the place where they are.

Most regions have licensed plant-rescue teams, - people who are notified when a builder is about to bulldoze a site where natives are known to be. Trish organized one in my township before a new parking lot was built for the high school. The rescue teams go in first and dig plants, collect seeds, and/or make cuttings to re-establish them elsewhere so they're not lost. Sometimes these are sold at plant sales and it's usually all right to buy these when you're sure of the source and the plants aren't too far away from their place of origin.

But there are disreputable plant dealers who plunder native landscapes, so it's best to buy your natives from someone you know, or look for a nursery specializing in native plants. By doing this, you'll know the plants have been propagated from divisions, cuttings or seeds that were gathered responsibly, and you'll know they're local genotypes. Once established, your native prairie will bring you so much pleasure that you'll say it was well worth the effort. The plant communities you've brought into your life will hum to you comfortingly with memories they carry in their genes.

Wild Genes

Last year Deanne, Judy and I took a trip to Bill Schneider's Native Plant Nursery. *(See Resources, Appendix A)* We saw small seedlings of Monardas fistulosa and punctata (wild bergamot and horsemint); Eupatoriums perfoliatum and maculatum (boneset and Joe-Pye Weed); Rudbeckias hirta and lacianata (black-eyed Susan and cut-leaved Coneflower); Andropogons, (bluestems); Hystrix patula (bottlebrush grass); and Solidagos (goldenrods), all lovingly propagated from hand-collected seeds, so that the parent plants are left in their places. We tried to imagine how they'd look full grown. We saw silky dogwood (Cornus amomum), shrubby cinquefoil, (Potentilla fruticosa), sycamore (Platanus occidentalis) and yellow birch (Betula alleghaniensis) - woody types known as "disturbance species" because they tend to gather where natural disturbance has taken place.

We saw native grasses, sedges and rushes. These are plants whose family roots go deep in Michigan soil. They know how to live well in this place and each one has a role to play in its ecological harmony. They know their neighbors and over centuries, have worked out ways of interacting with other native plants and with the wild birds, insects, and animals indigenous to this area. For example, the Luna moth needs the walnut; the zebra swallowtail needs the pawpaw; the cecropia moth and the coral hairstreak butterfly both need the wild cherry; the fritillary needs the violet; the swallowtail needs the spicebush (Lindera benzoin) and the butterflies known as the question mark, comma, tawny emperor and mourning cloak all need the hackberry (Celtis occidentalis). Chances are these native plants need the pollination services of these moths and butterflies as well. When the dodo bird went extinct, a tree that it depended on went into decline as well. This phenomenon, now known as the "dodo effect," demonstrates the reciprocity that functions between species of vastly different sorts.

Bill seemed willing to spend hours with us, discussing the plants and their ecosystems, answering all of our questions. I bought one plug each of five or six grasses and forbs. The idea was that by watching them grow, I'd become familiar with them at any stage of their growth.

On the way home, Deanne reflected on the experience: "Being in the midst of those ancient beings, you could almost hear them singing together. You could feel their genetic longevity; their wisdom, built up over eons of time. Those genes have been here, harmonizing with this place, for such a long, long time. They know so much."

PART III:

Exotics

CHAPTER 7:

Alien Invasions

The great destruction brought to our country
through foreign importations must prove
alarming to the future. Many of these importations
will in time become the sparrows of the plant
world and destructive to the beauty which is ours.

Jens Jensen, *Siftings*

Pond Management

The pond grasses are happy to see me coming, armed with scissors
and a long-handled scythe for the annual *pond-daylighting*. Cool-season
grasses that have adapted to wet feet, they've already set their seed and
await my assistance for the seed-dispersal that marks the fulfillment
of their raison d'être. The phragmites that dwell amongst them are
what I'm really after. They haven't yet developed their fecund plumes,
so cutting them now, before they go to seed, will be less futile. The
phragmites are reluctant, as I pull them toward me from the deeper
part of the pond with my dull scythe, good only for corralling deep-
water stickups.

I can't believe I'm doing this. And I can't believe I've done it every
June for eleven years. At first, I wade out only to a depth no higher than
the tops of my Wellingtons, believing I can stay dry. Even remembering
other years - even this year when the pond is exceptionally high - I
persist in this foolish belief, only to find myself committed to deeper
and deeper depths. The first rush of water over the tops of my boots

is shocking, but the water is warm, and after that I hardly notice, as knees, thighs, hips, and torso are soaked. Before I know it, I'm in pond-goo up to my armpits.

I covet my brother-in-law's waders, but deep down I know even they would probably fill up with water as I lose the love of dryness in favor of a determination to get every last phragmite before it goes to seed. Six hours later I cart the last wheelbarrow full of phragmite off to the mulch pile, reminding myself that at least it makes good mulch.

Every year, before I start, I wonder if this strenuous homage to the pond-god is really necessary. I want things natural, I remind myself. But natural means major pond-loss, intensified by the invasiveness of the phragmites, which are both the symptom and cause of this accelerated filling in with oxygen-depriving vegetation known as eutrophication.

It comes down to whether or not I want a pond; a wanting that diminishes every year. Without these heroics, you'd never know there's a pond there, or a lovely shaded clearing with a welcoming bench and a phlox garden with tall blue ageratum whose job it is to beckon visitors from across the pond. Failing such an invitation, a person might never venture down the path past the hosta bed and around the west side of the pond.

Yes, there really is a pond back there, but no one will ever see it if I do not perform the annual *pond-daylighting* ritual. Otherwise, there would be only a seemingly impenetrable screen of tall grass and phragmite, with a narrow path leading into it. So six hours later, wet with pond scum and who knows what else, I slosh toward the house where I shed my Wellies and jeans on the deck before entering the house for a shower. If I told people I did this they'd think I'm crazy. They'd be right. With *scissors!!???* they'd ask incredulously, before notifying family members.

Exotics (Aliens)

Phragmites. That lovely tall stuff you see in the ditches alongside the freeway, waving their white or black plumes at you as you drive by. They jam up wetlands; use up space that more ecologically benign native rushes might have occupied. They're a plague. Deanne, one of four women who are building a straw-bale house, values them for their reeds, which make good thatching material for the roof. The master thatcher they brought over here from Denmark to teach them the thatching craft told them he'd never before seen such fine thatching material. Deanne and her helpers go out every weekend in the fall to harvest phragmites. They have a permit from the Drain Commissioner in St. Clair County, which is overrun by Phragmites. I've invited her to bring her crew. Maybe if straw-bale houses were to become a fad, the wetlands could begin to function again as they should.

Where I live, phragmite (Phragmites australis) comes close in its perniciousness to purple loosestrife (Lythrum salicaria), an invasive, aggressive plant with beautiful tall spikey pink blossoms. Purple loosestrife and Phragmite are choking off Michigan wetlands at a terrifying rate.

We've all heard that development and sprawl are using up native habitat. In some places, development may at least be somewhat contained by zoning ordinances, and conservation easements. Phragmite and purple loosestrife, on the other hand, know no boundaries.

Purple Loosestrife

Before I moved here, I planted some purple loosestrife in my garden. I bought it at a nursery. *It seemed like a good idea at the time.* However, when I started hanging out with the people at *Wild Ones*. (See Appendix A, Resources.) I learned that purple loosestrife is one of the worst of the invasive exotics. Hordes of purple loosestrife are displacing the native wetland plants that wildlife need to thrive.

Purple Loosestrife plants average 2 - 3 million seeds per plant per year. These seeds remain viable for three years. Talk about prolific! Their beautiful pinkish-purple blossoms find their way into marshes and wetlands, completely taking over and elbowing out the other species that are trying to do the work of the wetland. Purple loosestrife, which some call "the purple plague" is a poor substitute for the native sedges and rushes they are replacing, natives that are geniuses at filtering evil stuff out of water and slowing down storm water runoff. Purple loosestrife is good at only these things: looking pretty, throwing seeds around promiscuously, and reproducing like gangbusters.

Up until just a few years ago, purple loosestrife was sold in Michigan nurseries. People may tell you there's a legal, sterile species that is still sold in nurseries. This "sterile" variety can crossbreed with other loosestrife nearby and produce viable seed. Like its exotic cousin, it cannot be sold legally in Michigan. Although the sale of purple loosestrife is now banned in Michigan, it is not yet banned in many other states.

As an alternative to purple loosestrife, many native landscapers have turned to the *Liatris aspera* and *spicata* (rough and marsh blazing stars) tall, spikey pink natives that have the same "look" as purple loosestrife.

A naturalist I know noticed some loosestrife growing in the Hula Nature Reserve in Israel, where he was visiting. Thinking he was doing them a favor, he pulled it out and victoriously presented it to the park ranger. To his embarrassment, he learned that in Israel, purple loosestrife is not an invasive exotic, but a *protected native!* In that place, it's kept in control naturally by a native beetle there, and by the other native insects, bacteria, soil type, and all the other native plants with which it evolved. It all depends on where you are.

Other Exotics

There are other plants, things we plant in our gardens that also contribute to the loss of wildlife habitat. Every time we plant an alien or exotic in our garden, we run the risk of contributing to this loss. Although there are many non-native cultivars that are not invasive and do not cause damage in the wild, the list of those that do is long. Reading through the list, I feel queasy, recognizing how many of these marauders I went to some trouble to obtain and plant in my garden before I knew better. Oriental bittersweet *(celastrus orbiculata);* lily of the valley *(convallaria majalis);* crown vetch *(coronilla varia);* baby's breath *(gypsophilia spp.);* honeysuckle *(Lonicera maaskii and tatarica);* Japanese knotweed *(polygonum cuspidatum),* and periwinkle *(vinca minor)* – these are among the worst. *It seemed like a good idea at the time.*

Simply put, an exotic plant, sometimes called an "alien" species, is anything that isn't a native. It has been estimated that over 2,000 new species have been introduced in the United States just in the last 100 years. Others would put that estimate much higher by an order of magnitude. The Nature Conservancy says that since the days of the European settlement, "more than 4,500 alien species have gained a foothold in the U.S."[31] They name alien species as the greatest threat to the 2500 listed imperiled or endangered species, second only to habitat destruction from sprawl.

Exotics that are opportunistic and invasive tend to take over in the wild, squeezing out native plants. These tough aliens do just fine in the absence of fertilizers and insecticides. The natural predators and diseases that might have kept them in check in their original bioregions are lacking. With nothing to hold them back, they overrun their new environs, recklessly reproducing and generally partying down until there is little or nothing left of the native communities that once were there. By taking over an ecosystem, they simplify it, weakening the entire system. They turn it into a monoculture where only one thing can grow, and thereby cause unimaginable loss of diverse native plant species and wildlife habitat.

> Joanne Wolf puts it in perspective:
> . . . A global horticultural industry and worldwide market now make it possible to acquire plants from around the world and to create hybrid varieties that are showier, uniquely colored, scentless, or otherwise genetically altered. But where are the plant's pollinators - the beetles, bees, butterflies, birds, and bats? When we import a plant from another continent, the life forms associated with it are not imported also, other than inadvertently. The plant is not genetically adapted to its new home and may be invasive or require high maintenance. Even more importantly, we must ask the question, what native, life-supporting vegetation are we removing to plant unadapted or invasive vegetation?[32]

Plants that look nice in your yard, such as ground Ivy *(Glechoma hederacea)* can escape into the surrounding countryside and take over native habitats that are beneficial to wildlife and other native plants. In Michigan alone, 30% of the state's 2,600 plant species are aliens that have become naturalized, i.e., they are capable of establishing and maintaining themselves without our care.[33]

While many of these are not a problem, the invasive ones are causing serious disruption in local ecosystems. The result of these infestations is the unraveling of rich ecosystems that once held a great diversity of native flora. What remains are large patches of single species monocultures, which do not, as a rule, offer good food sources for wildlife, - certainly not the variety required by wildlife for its fullest vigor.

To get a sense of the magnitude of this problem, consider the words of Peter Russell: "Current estimates suggest that species are disappearing at the rate of one per hour or perhaps faster. At this rate, more than half of the earth's plant and animal species will have been eliminated within the next few hundred years."[34] Russell feels it will probably be much sooner than that, because our potential for destruction increases with technological progress. The invasion of exotic species accounts for an extremely large proportion of this loss in both plant and animal kingdoms.

According to the World Conservation Union, one out of eight native plant species is now at risk. Each one is an essential component of its ecosystem which will also disappear. The animals whose lives are woven into these disappearing ecosystems are also at risk, as they find their food sources dwindling.

And it's not just the food-sources for wildlife that are disappearing. Following a six-year study, scientists at the Morton Arboretum near Chicago have determined that songbirds are now more vulnerable to predators because the exotic plants that are taking over much of the undeveloped landscape do not afford favorable nesting conditions. "The major contributing factor to declining bird populations," says Joe Johnson of the Kellogg Bird Sanctuary in Michigan, "is habitat loss and modification." Ground-nesting birds have an even tougher time, finding no protection at all in turfgrass, like my New Jersey killdeer.

Aside from the loss of so many of our furry and feathered friends, these ecosystems make up the "rich diversity of life that underpins everything from food production to a host of essential medicines."[35] Alien plants are deeply implicated in this loss. Additionally, non-natives in the wild are creating "fuel" for out-of-control wild fires in areas where prescribed burns are not allowed.

These exotic escapees from our gardens are sometimes called "fugitives," conjuring up images of stealth and skullduggery. With collars turned up and hat brims down, they've slipped out of the comfort of our garden-prisons to go out and raise a ruckus in the wild. These feral plants often fare better in the wild, where no one will pull them or cut them back if they get out of hand. In my neck of the woods the most common "bad guys" are Japanese honeysuckle *(Lonicera japonica);* glossy buckthorn *(Rhamnus' cathartica) and frangula)* barberry (Berberis sp) - yes, those nice, thorny, red-leaved hedge-plants); autumn olive *(Eleagnus umbrellatta);* tree of heaven *(Ailanthus altissima);* spotted knapweed *(Centaurea maculosa);* phragmite *(Phragmites australis)* and of course, the dreaded purple loosestrife, (Lythrum salicaria).

Many of these exotic species, such as the multiflora rose, (Rosa multiflora), and autumn olive *(Eleagnus umbrellatta)* were introduced by agricultural extension services to be used as natural fences and windbreaks, and for erosion control. *It seemed like a good idea at the time.* Many are still being sold in nurseries.

All of us are guilty. We didn't know any better. I felt terrible when I hacked my Asian honeysuckle *(Lonicera xbella)* to the root. It had provided a welcome cooling service to my house. The birds loved it. They loved it so much, they were seeding the whole neighborhood with *Lonicera xbella,* which was showing up in the woods next door, where it didn't belong. That's how it happens, with a planting in your yard that seems innocent enough in the beginning. I've replaced the honeysuckle with a native redbud *(Cercis Canadensis)* and a native serviceberry *(Amelanchier spicata).* It cost me $300. A heavy price for ecological virtue, I thought.

Weeds

When I first started gardening, my love of growing things was indiscriminate. It seemed to me that weeds had as much right to grow as flowers and vegetables did. Then I read Michael Pollan's book, *Second Nature* where I learned that weeds have evolved along with human cultivation, opportunistically seeking out newly disturbed soil. They do not grow in nearly as much abundance in an undisturbed field as they do in your garden. Weeds are, Pollan reminds us, "truly a different order or being, more versatile, better equipped, swifter, craftier" than other garden plants. It's not merely a matter of accidental encroachment. Your garden is exactly where a weed wants to be.

Weeds are not wild. They are not natives, though unplanned natives may occasionally show up in your garden. The uninvited dandelions, crab grass, lamb's-quarters, daisies, the Queen Anne's lace and mullein pulled out by people in the Midwest were brought here on purpose or by accident by the Europeans who colonized North

America. Counterstrategies have been developed to fight the clever survival techniques so cunningly evolved by these weeds, and these counterstrategies constitute the bulk of a gardener's work. They also constitute the bulk of the herbicide industry's business. Weeds are here because we are here. No gardens, no weeds.

After reading Pollan's book, my attitude toward weeds changed. I no longer think of them as wayward children who need understanding. I hadn't known that weeds are exotics too; ones that are adapted to human cultivation. Like purple loosestrife, they're uninvited guests with no respect for their host's sensibilities.

CHAPTER 8:

Vegetative Warfare

Learning about loosestrife was my introduction to an internecine vegetative war in which humans are implicating themselves, and a concept I still haven't fully digested: the idea that in the plant world, there are, as they say in *Wild Ones*, good guys and bad guys. Natives are the good guys and invasive exotics are the bad guys. Natives can be invasive too, but a native monoculture is a rarity. In a diverse ecosystem, those natives that tend to proliferate are almost always kept in check by predators and other natives.

I also learned that there are veritable armies of people who go out every weekend to pull, burn, whack, poison, etc. - whatever it takes to obliterate the bad guys (exotics), while planting and encouraging the good guys (natives).

One of the armaments in this war is known as *the glove of death*, - a latex glove, over which a cotton glove is worn by the combatant. The cotton glove is soaked in a powerful herb*icide* (notice the syllable), then stroked on the leaves of the loosestrife plant. This was more than I wanted to know. The image of these gentle ladies and men, lovers of the natural world whose hearts are more ecological than mine, slogging through wetland areas in their Wellingtons and hip boots, applying the *glove of death* to these lovely flowering plants can be a headache-causing cognitive dissonance. But this is a very serious war.

In 1994, the galerucella beetle was discovered to have an appetite for purple loosestrife. Thousands of these beetles are now being raised in captivity and released in areas where the loosestrife is asserting itself. The beetles eat the buds, stems, and leaves of the plant, preventing seed production and eventually leading to the plant's demise. It seems to be effective. So far, so good. While to my mind it seems preferable to the *Glove of Death,* I wonder what this beetle will eat if and when all the purple loosestrife is gone. Will it be another case of *It seemed like a good idea at the time?* I hope and trust they know what they're doing.

Purple loosestrife is one of the bad guys. In dark alleys, it conspires with Norway maple, *(Acer patanoides);* ground ivy *(Glechoma hederacea)*; and *myrtle (Vinca minor)* to take over the Midwest landscape and vanquish the natives. Marching orders against them allow no prisoners to be taken. A merciless scorched earth (in some cases, a scorched wetland) policy is in place.

Sometimes the scorched-earth policy is literal. Flame throwers have been used for precision elimination of invasive aliens, selectively taking them out while leaving the natives. While not as selective, prescribed burns are perhaps even more effective for controlling invasive exotics, whose seeds cannot survive the heat. In earlier times, native plants, which evolved with the disturbance of fire, were revived, and exotic ones were controlled in this way. But in recent years, with human populations moving more and more into unoccupied land, burning is often regarded as hazardous and the natural or unnatural fires, which might have kept the invasive aliens in check, are put out as soon as possible. Fire suppression is now recognized as one of the most important causes of wildlife habitat loss.

Not all bad guys started out that way. Some, well-behaved at first, have lately been proven to kick up their heels in the wild, where there are no watchful eyes to curb their aggression. Botanists are now beginning to think more pro-actively, trying to predict which commonly used garden plants might *become* invasive 50 years from now. Dispensability is one criterion for this determination. Is it self-sowing? Does it set seeds quickly?   How prolifically are seeds set; how many ways does it have of spreading quickly? These are questions that are asked. Growth features, such as the rate of growth, strong response to fertilizer, crowding of other plants, density, height, early germination, and frost resistance are also taken into consideration. Ecological amplitude - (does it thrive everywhere?) - counts as well, and so do genetic features that place it in a different family of genus than some native plants, making tempering competition unlikely.

If the Soil Conservation Service (now the Natural Resource Conservation Service) and conservation districts had applied such criteria to autumn olive years ago, I might not have had the following experience:

Autumn Olive Pogrom

They showed up the second year, nice, shapely, shrubby plants with silvery undersided leaves. Strong, healthy, with a will to live, these lovely bushes that would eventually turn into low, well-branching trees, eagerly stepped up to the job of providing understory. They provided cover for the animals I wanted to welcome, and late summer berries for the birds. I loved them.

Then I found out what they were, and got wind of their sullied reputation. It took me a while to grasp the concept that autumn olive is really bad. That's what happens when you don't want to know the names of things.

Autumn Olive was sold as a cover for wildlife by agricultural extension services in the upper Midwest before they knew better. Like the multiflora rose in New Jersey and other Eastern states, it runs rampant, squeezing out native plants (the ones we want). Autumn olive, along with phragmite, purple loosestrife, glossy buckthorn, and the multiflora rose is an aggressive, hard-to-arrest hoodlum of the plant world.

I never imagined when I decided to encourage wildlife by letting things go, that I'd be in the position of having to pull stuff out. And autumn olive is almost impossible to pull out. By the time I realized I'd have to do something about it, many of the bushes were turning into trees, enjoying a free ride.

I heard that you can get rid of them by cutting them back twice in the same season. Makes sense to me. But the person sitting next to the person who told me this said it doesn't work. The only way to get rid of autumn olive, he insisted, is by sponging herbicide on all the stumps after cutting it back. Others, speaking from experience, have corroborated his advice.

I resolved to try the *cut-back-twice-in-the-same-year* method, which seemed easier than digging, and more ecological than poisoning. Yesterday my autumn olive pogrom began. I had no idea how bad it would make me feel. Each tree I lopped off at the root protested the atrocity. "Look how well we're growing!" they cried, "Look at our lovely leaves. See their beautiful silvery undersides. See these green berries? In another three or four weeks, they'll be juicy and orange. We've been working all year to produce them. They're just getting started! What do you think you're doing?"

Turning a deaf ear, I resolutely cut down all the ones in the front of the house, and then moved to the back. Ruthlessly I lopped, hacked and dragged them off to the brush pile. They have thorns. I forgave them the scratches I sustained in the carnage. They were only trying to defend themselves, as anyone would. They were entitled to a few scratches after what I'd done to them.

I remembered the Trees-of-Heaven my friend Clark freed from the barbed wire that was cutting into their trunks. He told me about communing with them in the middle of the night, out there on the island, where his father had planted them decades before. People had been telling Clark how invasive they are, - how, if he didn't get rid of them they'd eventually take over everything. But he talked to the Trees-of-Heaven and they had a different take on things. It seemed to Clark (or so the conniving trees told him), that if he didn't cut them down they would stay confined to the island where they wouldn't bother anybody. So he let them stay. I briefly wondered if I could make such a deal with the autumn olive. But as I looked at them springing up everywhere, it was clear to me they had no intention of staying confined anywhere.

I don't know if cutting them back twice in the same season will do it, but honoring my vow to dig as little as possible, and eschewing *-cides*, it seemed to be the only recourse. Now they're gone. The place does look neater, more open. But I miss them. And I suppose I shall be lopping autumn olive for the rest of my life.

Managing Exotics

This brings up another unpleasant reality. I now know that doing nothing is not the best strategy. I thought I could get away with minimal mowing and a few garden beds. Let nature do the rest. But like so many other situations in the modern world, we've painted ourselves into a corner where, as Wendell Berry puts it, it's too late now to do nothing. Like Berry, Michael Pollan recognized, after his attempts to just "harmonize with nature," that we now must make informed choices, "discriminate between good and bad, apply our intelligence and sweat to the earth. . . Mere neglect won't bring back nature," he concludes. [36]

We now have a responsibility toward the natural world that requires conscience, ethical decisions, and conscious choice. Perhaps this is what was meant when our shallow "knowledge," that forbidden fruit we ate with such guilt, led to our eviction from the Garden of Eden. Perhaps this was the reason we would henceforth have to live by the sweat of our brow.

Government Initiatives

Alien plants cost the United States more than $7 billion annually in crop and rangeland losses. In 1999, President Clinton created the Invasive Species Council, an interagency group to strategize ways to stem the tide of alien species that are threatening to destroy so many of our valuable ecosystems. Their mandate is to prepare a national invasive species management plan to combat the spread of alien species.[37] In 2000, the Union of Concerned Scientists began their own new initiative to monitor the Council's work and develop ways to link the scientific community with policymakers who are working on this issue.

The grasses that I continue to mow – my paths and clearings - are not native. These grasses were introduced from Europe, Asia, South America, Southeast Asia and Africa. I wonder if they'll show up sometime in the national invasive species management plan. These are the grasses that predominate in my supposedly "wild" landscape, where I stopped mowing over eight years ago. To have a truly native landscape would require more work than I'm willing, at this point, to do.

CHAPTER 9:

Learning Curve

To have a truly a native landscape, I'd need to do a full-blown restoration. To find out if there's anything here to restore all of the landforms, hydrology, soil conditions, natural features, corridor-connections, and existing natives on my property would have to be inventoried by a knowledgeable consultant.

That's only the beginning. Some purists, as described in Chapter 6, recommend ripping out or poisoning everything (including the lawn), that isn't a native, and starting over with only natives. While I admire the people who are willing to go to such lengths, replacing their lawns with native wildflower meadows and native prairies, I'm looking for some sort of rapprochement with my property. I'm looking, at this point, for natural landscaping, not restoration.

Although my property is still dominated by non-native grasses, a few natives have, no doubt, found their way back into the areas I stopped mowing, regenerating themselves there. But not being able to identify them, I had no idea they were there. I would often come home from a native plant sale to find the native plant I had just paid good money for, already growing right here, under my nose. That's why I started planting plugs of natives here and there, labeling them as best I could. This way, I reasoned, I could track their appearance and habits as they grow to maturity, and become familiar with each species; better able to identify what's already here.

My first attempts did not go well. I put plugs in the wrong places, or just plunked them down where lots of other things were growing. I disregarded Bill Schneider's rule about planting whole communities of natives, not just a few here and there. Now I can't find them. Their labels have disappeared, or they've been taken over by more aggressive neighbors. Before the plugs, I tried to plant a "wildflower" bed, - you know, the kind that comes in a can. My naiveté with "wildflowers" permeates these initial endeavors, recorded in my gardening journal:

> The wildflower garden is a free-for-all. Everything is vying
> for position, elbowing each other out. Before I threw the
> wildflower seeds in, I planted some lavender. Never saw
> it again. In spring and early summer, the bed is quite
> tame, almost domestic, with bright poppies and wild
> daisies singing together in two-part harmony. But by
> late summer, it's every plant for itself. The first year,
> the Black-eyed Susan was the Great Pioneer and
> definitely the winner, with bachelor buttons and small,
> unknown (to me) forbs dotting the garden appealingly.
> This year, the Black-eyed Susan is nowhere to be seen
> and the yarrow has emerged as the Macho Grande *Big
> Winnah* of the wildflower bed; the wildest of all wildflowers.
> By mid-August, even that's falling over and brown. It's a
> big mess.

I now know that yarrow *(Achillea millefolium)* isn't a native wildflower. Most of the things in my "wildflower" mix were not native to this area. Many, like the yarrow, are invasive exotics. (Trish, where were you when I needed you?) The proper way to have done this would have been to hire a native plant consultant to do an assessment of what's already here, and what plant communities would do best in each of the micro-conditions on my property: areas where sun, shade, and soil conditions favor certain types of plants. Watching plugs grow is the slow way, and it's easy to lose track of what you're doing. Now I see that it would have been better then to have had some sort of plan.

Last year, before I planted my new "native bed," I drew it on paper first. I hung the bed-map on my kitchen wall and lived with it over the winter, tinkering with it now and then. I chose plants from Bill Schneider's nursery that were suited to full sun and compatible with each other. A few exotics were left in their places, ones that aren't invasive, but the new plants were all local natives.

The new bed just went nuts. I couldn't believe the variety and vigor of the plants that reached their full maturity, even in the first year. The butterflies that showed up were so plentiful and of such variety that I bought a butterfly field guide to keep up with them. Although it's not a truly native landscape, as it would be if I'd done a restoration, it's immensely satisfying. I can hardly wait until next year, when I can do the same thing in the shady wooded area in my back yard, with shade-loving natives.

It takes some effort to get up to speed on natives and aliens, partly because these things are not yet widely known. Certainly the threat posed to wildlife by growing alien species in our gardens is just barely making it into an occasional headline, and is often seen as controversial. The only reason for this controversy that makes sense is the challenge posed by native landscaping to a traditional aesthetic. That, and the huge investment on the part of the horticulture industry, which is motivated to keep exotics moving into home gardens.

Some native landscape proponents have been trying to nudge local nurseries to carry local genotype natives, - providing them with stickers and identifying posters, so the natives these nurseries do stock can be easily identified by their customers. But large-scale wholesale sources for natives are still hard to find, and there's too much money to be made pushing exotics to expect much change to come through nurseries any time soon.

For the home gardener, devotion to natives will be literally a grass roots initiative for some time to come. It will take continued diligence to find reliable local sources for native plants, and superhuman sales resistance when the catalogs start appearing in gardeners' mail boxes in February. Resisting the large, colorful, (and often invasive) blooms they see in those catalogs, and in most nurseries, will take character and determination. Nurseries stock what people ask for, and what they can get. Perhaps as more people ask for natives, they may become more widely available. And it may get easier as government initiatives begin to have some impact. These will be discussed later. Until then, native landscapers will have to seek out local growers who specialize in local native genotypes.

Genetically Modified Organisms (GMOs)

"Alleging the firm's seeds have contaminated (his) organic fields,"[38] an organic farmer in Saskatchewan, has joined a class-action lawsuit against *Monsanto* and *Aventis*. The lawsuit seeks compensation for damages caused by Monsanto and Aventis' genetically engineered (GE) canola, and an injunction to prevent Monsanto from introducing GE wheat in Saskatchewan.

In November, 2001, scientists reported "finding genes from GM corn in Mexican 'cirollo maize,' a source of modern corn varieties. Plant breeders worry such cross-pollination could flood out genetic diversity, making it impossible to breed new strains."[39] Many organic farmers, as well as plant-breeders, are understandably concerned.

Agriculture's newest magic bullet is invading the wild as well. As if the spread of exotic species were not enough, genetically modified organisms (GMOs) have introduced a new threat to wildlife habitat. With the rapid advancements biotechnology, genetically altered crops are being rushed to market with inadequate testing and some are already having a deleterious effect on wildlife.

Bt corn was developed to carry a gene found in Bt, a natural insecticide often used by organic farmers. Not only is there the danger of its widespread use resulting in harmful insects developing resistance to Bt, rendering it useless to organic farmers, many are worried about its unintended consequences in the wild as well. "When the Bt-corn threat to the monarch butterfly hit the pages of the *New York Times* in 2000, it set off a blizzard of publicity about the environmental risks of Bt crops and other genetically engineered organisms released into the environment."[40] It seems the pollen from the genetically modified corn, toxic to the monarch caterpillar, had blown and fallen on the leaves of the milkweed that the monarch relies on as its major food-source. The implications were staggering.

Soybeans that have been genetically modified to be *Roundup* tolerant are already on the market and have gotten there with inadequate testing for long-term health problems, both for the humans who eat them and the other plants growing in their vicinity. What about new proteins that cause allergies? What about the development of resistance to pesticides, and the possible spread of traits that shouldn't be spread?

By 1999, half of all soybeans grown in the U.S. had been genetically altered. One might well wonder why, when a 1999 U.S. Department of Agriculture (USDA) study of more than 8,000 field trials found that Monsanto's *Roundup Ready* soybean seeds produced *lower* yields than non-engineered seeds,"[41] (emphasis mine).

"35 percent of all corn and nearly half of all cotton are now genetically modified and unidentified as such." Now, "genetically modified organisms (GMOs) are showing up in products ranging from baby formulas to tortilla chips."[42] Other genetically altered crop seeds are entering the market and being shipped overseas, where farmers in third-world countries have been persuaded that their yields will increase. This, despite a 1998 study by the USDA finding that "66 percent of genetically engineered seeds produced no significant differences in crop yield."[43]

Beyond the threat to genetic diversity and the contamination of native species, the social and political consequences of GM crops could be monumental. Customer choice (labeling) and corporate control of the food supply are just two of the many ethical issues that cluster around genetically modified organisms. The law of unintended consequences has already asserted itself, and many are already saying *it seemed like a good idea at the time . . .*

Following the accidental mixing of GM foods with non-GM, *Archer Daniels Midland* farmers must segregate all GM produce from non-GM food. *Monsanto* gained notoriety with the development of the "terminator" seed, (seed-stock that has been genetically altered to be sterile, so that farmers who use it cannot save seeds from one year to the next). Their top executives, and those of *AstraZeneca, Aventis, DuPont* and *Novartis*, are worried about their market in Europe, where genetically modified crops can no longer be imported without E. U. approval. In the U. K., where protests against GM crops have turned ugly, McDonalds restaurants no longer sell genetically modified foods. "Food producers such as Nestle, Unilever, and Cadbury have agreed not to include genetically modified ingredients in products they sell in certain countries. Japan, South Korea, New Zealand, and Austria have all implemented mandatory labeling laws."[44]

Here in the U.S., GM food is still primarily a labeling issue, although some U. S. companies, such as Gerber, Iams, Grupo Maseca and CASCO, have "voluntarily committed to not using genetically modified crops in some or all of their products."[45] In 1999, Monsanto terminated the terminator, closing down its research.

Work is now underway to develop a genetically engineered lawn grass that won't need to be mowed. Pretty colors are being developed too. Not only can you have a perfectly even, weed-free lawn, you can have a purple lawn, or mauve. You can have a lawn that glows in the dark when you step on it. Even though The American Society of Landscape Architects has joined environmentalists in calling upon the USDA to suspend all field tests on genetically engineered grasses, the research continues apace.

Other garden cultivars are similarly being genetically engineered for more desirable characteristics, such as releasing their scent only in the evening, when most people are coming home.[46] Never mind that the beneficial insects, who rely on scent to tell them where the pollen is, will be thrown off. Most of these cultivars are sterile anyway. Never mind that poison pollen from one plant can kill the very insects that are needed by another plant to reproduce. The cynically "important" thing is that we humans get maximum enjoyment from these "products".

This kind of short-sighted tinkering strikes at the very heart of the delicately balanced interrelationships in the natural world that have evolved over millennia, and is no less heinous than the idea of developing sterile crops so that indigenous farmers cannot save seeds from one year to the next. In an ABC News *Nightline* report (July 21, 2000), Peter Jennings warned that the coming "wall of gene-pollution may be an even bigger threat than the threat to our food supply." The threat of gene pollution is different from chemical pollution, which does eventually, over millennia, disperse. This is, as Michael Pollan points out, "more like a disease."[47] It is time, some say, for a *Genetic Bill of Rights. (See Appendix B.)*

Soul Modification

We have come, it seems, to a zone of "terrible freedoms" and ferocious progress; a place where our marvelous strategies for survival and comfort are turning on us. It is not just the natural world around us that is eroding away. Our souls are experiencing increasing diminishment as well.

Developing an appreciation of native vegetation and striving to eliminate invasive aliens from our properties may be the first step in our comprehension of the complicated relationships that constitute healthy ecosystems. As we cultivate a deeper relationship with the wildness out there, we'll find a new, safe, and nourishing wildness animating our inner lives as well, reminding us that we are part of a complex and beautiful web of interdependency in which all life-forms are interlinked with each other.

Natural landscaping concretizes the theoretical concepts ecologists have been telling us about. It makes real the interconnectivity and inner radiance of nature. It helps us to know how it all works together, with the intention of the berry sharing equal significance with the intention of the junco who eats it. It roots us deeply in the present, and binds us back to the past in profound ways. It satisfies our hankering for the feeling of belonging in this "place where I am." It gives us a sense of continuance, broader and deeper than mere sustainability. In this place the material and the spiritual are mixed and simmered together in a rich broth to be savored and sipped, given and gulped with greedy pleasure.

Natural landscaping teaches us about reciprocity. In a workshop with Thomas Raincrowe, Poet and founder of *Katuah Journal: A Bioregional Journal,* he suggested that we each ask ourselves the question, "Why am I here?" and write the answer with our non-dominant hand. Expecting a more ultimate kind of answer having to do with the purpose of my life, I was surprised and moved by what got written. "You are here," my left hand wrote, "because *this is the place that cares for you.*" It had never before occurred to me that a *place* – the land and its plants and animals – might possess the attribute of caring, but indeed, that has been my experience of this place. Caring *is*, indeed, reciprocal.

If we want to end our war with the natural world, it's time to see ourselves as part of nature, with common interests, needs and desires. "To live consciously in the midst of wild things is to live in the midst of soul," Philip Simons reminds us. [48] Natural landscaping may not be the whole answer, but it's one part - a very important part in restoring our broken world.

PART IV:

Natural Landscaping
- Then and Now

CHAPTER 10:

Jens Jensen: Native Landscape Prophet

Landscaping is a composition of life
that unfolds a mysterious beauty
from time to time until a mature age.

Jens Jensen, *Siftings*

Background and Influences

Natural landscapes. Native plants. Backyard wildlife habitat. These are not new ideas. Although the passion with which they're being embraced today by ordinary property owners nationwide is refreshing and invigorating, these ideas were deeply prefigured by a landscape architect who was extremely active in the late 1800s and early 1900s.

Jens Jensen came to America from Denmark when he was in his twenties. He'd been schooled in one of the Danish folk schools, which had been established as a way of preserving Danish heritage and liberal Christian values in the face of German occupation. From this, he had learned an appreciation of the natural world along with his academic studies. With an emphasis on "education for life," classes were often held outdoors. Campfires and festivals, whose origins dated back to pagan days, were frequent occurrences. These reinforced for Jensen memories of growing up on the family farm, with its untrimmed hedges abundant with native life, and trips taken with his father and brothers to find wildflowers on the ocean bluffs.[49]

After Folk School, Jensen attended Tune Agricultural School near Copenhagen, where he learned the technical aspects of agriculture. Here, as in Folk School, the understanding of the locality and the region were stressed. The soil itself was emphasized as "the source of all life".[50]

Before coming to America, while reluctantly serving in the German army under Prussian rule, Jensen saw the "French Garden" and "English Garden" parks in Berlin. The contrast between these two styles made a strong impression on Jensen. The English garden, he wrote in *Siftings*, expressed a "sense of freedom . . . in keeping with the life of the people." By contrast, he thought the French gardens with their straight lines and ostentation were expressions of a "pompous monarchy". He associated their strict geometry with repression, royalty and despotic government. Jensen loved long, flowing, gentle curves, and felt they were more natural than straight lines. "Straight lines," he said, "spell autocracy, of which most European gardens are an expression, and their course points to intellectual decay, which soon develops a prison from which the mind can never escape." [51]

Although he'd grown up in a prosperous family, Jensen saw the injustices of foreign occupation, and had a keen sense of social justice. Beneath the carefully tended overly ornamented French gardens he saw the labor of those less fortunate than the owners. He railed against the oppression of the lower classes by the ruling classes and compassionately sought ways to rectify these injustices through his work. Over the coming decades, his conservation sensibility would mature; his comprehension of native ecosystems would become more refined.

Although I've not found any evidence of this, Jensen may also have been influenced by Gertrude Jekyll, affectionately known in her later years as "Aunt Bumps." (Or maybe she was influenced by Jensen.) Aunt Bumps was a crusty English woman of the late 1800's who popularized the English cottage garden and the perennial border, emphasizing randomness and the use of plants adapted to local conditions. Jekyll and her mentor, William Robinson, favored "wild" or "natural" gardens over the formal gardens that predominated in Europe at that time. Both especially disliked the use of plants to further geometry or architectural features. Jekyll wrote:

The first purpose of a garden is to give happiness and
repose of mind, which is more often enjoyed in the
contemplation of the homely border . . . than in any of
those great gardens where the flowers lose their identity,
and with it their hold on the human heart, and have to take
a lower rank as mere masses of color filling so many
square yards of space.[52]

Whether or not they were known to one another, Jekyll's and
Jensen's ideas would work together synergistically to establish a new
gardening sensibility in the English-speaking world.

By the time he'd left Denmark to marry a woman from the
"cottage class", Jensen was primed for American democracy. He fell
in love with it and forever after expressed that love in his designs for
public places. He wanted to make green places available to the urban
poor near their homes for the refreshment of their souls. Although best
known for his park and estate work, he advocated kitchen gardens and
community gardens so people could grow their own food. This came
from his conviction of the health-giving properties of gardening, as
well as his desire to see people well fed. Jensen's social consciousness
was doubtless reinforced by his exposure, in the late 1890's and early
1900's to Jane Addams' Hull House. There, his sense of social justice
was honed. And there, also, the emphasis on the arts, so like the Folk
School of his youth, influenced his later passion for pageantry.

While he did develop hundreds of landscape designs for the estates
of wealthy Americans, Jensen did so primarily out of necessity, and
always thought of himself as a designer of public places.

The greatest portion of Jensen's work was done in Illinois, and
particularly in the Chicago area, where he designed parts of Humbolt
and Columbus Parks, as well as many others. When Jensen arrived in
Chicago in 1886, the city already had a rich history of park development
and land preservation. Dating back before the 1871 Chicago fire,
extensive park systems, green belts and boulevards had been envisioned
by Frederick Law Olmsted, Calvert Vaux, H.W.S Cleveland and other
landscaping exemplars. Olmsted held three elements to be essential to
any park: turf, foliage, and still water.

Jensen's Landscape Ethic

Olmsted and Cleveland had both argued for "natural scenery" in Chicago's parks, and the central feature of Washington Park was 100 acres of "flat, smooth turf, a bit of real prairie," a feature which Jensen would admire greatly and imitate frequently in his own park designs. One might speculate on the extent to which these greenswards of "flat smooth turf," might have been imprinted on the American psyche, reinforcing and fusing the image of the feudal "laund" (described in the introduction), with this artifact of the American prairie.

The American prairie was particularly inspiring for Jensen, its vast expanses reminding him of the flat surface of the sea he'd grown accustomed to near Denmark. He acknowledged that, like the sea, these prairies had "the distinct power of drawing one out, of arousing one's curiosity to investigate what is beyond the horizon." Often Jensen's Midwestern landscapes would rely on the flat plane of the hawthorn tree, one of his favorite native trees, to echo the flat plane of the prairie. Stratified rocks were often found in his landscapes as well, for the same purpose.

His heartstrings resonated to the wild roses, sweet flag and blackberries he saw by the edges of America's wetlands, which were so like the plants he remembered from his childhood in Denmark, and his appreciation of pre-European settlement American native plant communities developed as his style matured.

In his early landscapes, Jensen did cooperate in his clients' desires for formal gardens, with their geometric designs and manicured flower areas planted with imported, and later, hybrid varieties, an activity which he would later come to regret as "the folly of my youth." But he gradually allowed more and more expression of his attraction to native plants to enter his park work.

Although Aldo Leopold would later be credited with the first urban natural landscape, Jensen claimed to have created the first "American Garden" in 1888, in Chicago's Union Park. "The garden, a collection of native perennials set against a background of native trees and shrubs, marked the first of Jensen's major public landscape designs."[53] Jensen describes how this was done:

> I had a great collection of perennial wild flowers. We couldn't get the stock from nurserymen, as there had never been any requests for it, and we went out into the woods with a team

and wagon, and carted it in ourselves. Each plant was given room to grow as it wanted to. People enjoyed seeing the garden. They exclaimed excitedly when they saw flowers they recognized;they welcomed them as they would a friend from home. This was the first natural garden in Chicago, and as far as I know, the first natural garden in any large park in the country. To my delight the transplantings flourished and after a while I did away with formal beds.[54]

Present-day native landscapers will recognize the difficulty Jensen had in finding native plants at local nurseries. We too, often have difficulty finding the natives we want to plant, and, although not with team and wagon, we often have to travel some distance to find them. Without a rescue permit, we can't just dig them out of the nearest woods, as Jensen did. Even seed collection should be done in the wild only by reputable nursery persons who have permission from the landowner. Nurseries that specialize in native plants are propagating them as fast as they can to be ready to supply local nurseries when the demand for native plants increases, as it assuredly will. In the meantime, home landscapers are ethically bound to purchase stock only from permitted rescue teams or those growers who specialize in native plants, to discourage unauthorized plundering of wild native stock.

Jensen's "doing away with formal beds" did not happen all at once. He continued to design formal gardens for Chicago's Garfield and Humboldt Parks and for his many estate clients, only gradually changing over to predominately native plantings.

Olmsted apparently was not the purist Jensen was. Although Olmsted and Cleveland had utilized "naturalistic" forms in their work, they did not give the same attention to local plant associations that Jensen did, nor did they place as much importance on a plant's suitability to a particular soil type or region. So even though Olmsted's naturalistic style suggested something more in keeping with local flora than the formal gardens that were still prevalent in many American parks, and his name was often associated with native plantings, his vision of "natural" was not as refined as Jensen's was. In fact, Olmsted is credited (or blamed) with having introduced into the U. S. a number of invasive exotics, such as Japanese knotweed, (Polygonum cuspidatum).

Jensen utilized his landscape designs as teaching tools to help people appreciate the natural heritage of their Midwestern landscape, and he delighted in elevating "common" plants like sumac, goldenrod and elderberries to a new level of respect.

Creating *The American Garden* in 1888 had planted the seed of an idea in Jensen's psyche and perhaps the psyche of America as well. That idea would grow and flourish in the coming years. Jensen's own style would mature into a greater concern for native plant communities whose unique combinations, repeated again and again, distinguished a particular region. As well, he came to appreciate the zones of transition that exist between these plant communities. He would more and more eschew the imported "exotic" varieties and hybrids found in formal gardens. Eventually the formal "show" gardens which Jensen associated with European imperialism, became so repugnant to him that it catalyzed a colossal blow-up between him and Henry Ford's wife, Clara, who insisted on formal rose gardens at the Fords' Fair Lane estate in Dearborn, Michigan.

Wilhelm Miller, who credited Ossian Cole Simonds and Jensen as the founders of the Prairie style of landscape architecture, took the style further, suggesting that every town create its own version of it. In Miller's manifesto, *The Prairie Spirit*, he gave this impassioned proclamation:

> . . . I will try to open the eyes of those who can see
> no beauty in the common "brush" and wild flowers beside
> the country roads. If any souls have been deadened by sordid
> materialism I will stand with these people on the highest spot
> that overlooks a sea of rolling land where they can drink in the
> spirit of the prairies.
> I will fight to the last the greed that would destroy all
> native beauty. I will help my state establish and maintain a
> prairie park, which will restore for the delight of future
> generations some fragment of wild prairie - the source
> of our wealth and civilization.
> I will plant against the foundations of my house some
> bushes that will remind me of the prairie and be to my townsfolk
> a living symbol of the indomitable prairie spirit.[55]

Prairies

Prairies are open grasslands dominated by native perennial grasses and forbs. Fire, soil type and hydrology are the primary determinants of the different plant communities that are found in a prairie system. The primary landscape feature in the Midwest, and particularly in Illinois and Wisconsin, where Jensen did the majority of his work, is the prairie.

As I've mentioned, Jensen had a special place in his heart for prairies, those ecosystems that were once so typical of America's Midwest, where native grasses and wildflowers predominated. Wet prairies, dry prairies, dry mesic prairies (between wet and dry but more dry than wet) prairies, wet mesic prairies (more wet than dry), tallgrass and shortgrass prairies - all of them together formed a kind of prairie consciousness for Jensen, and others who shared his enthusiasm. Jensen and Ossian Cole Simonds, who were leaders of the Prairie style of landscape architecture, were both members of *The Cliffdwellers*, a downtown club of prominent Chicago men that included the prairie style architects, the most notable of whom was Frank Lloyd Wright. Like Wright, Simonds and Jensen both "insisted on design forms and materials that related directly to the surrounding region." Both became "ardent champions of the flora and subtle landforms of the prairie region."[56] They loved the region's flatness and its openness, and felt that a spirit was expressed there that could be found nowhere else in the world.

The prairie landscaping style, according to Wilhelm Miller, consists of three design principles: conservation (or preservation), restoration, and repetition (of the horizontal lines typical of the land or sky of the Midwestern prairie.)

Another important influence in Jensen's life was his lifelong friend, Frank Waugh, whose philosophy of the links between landscape and social influences was well articulated. Waugh could excuse the formalism found in the gardens of America's pioneers as indicative of the "constant struggle with nature" experienced by our early settlers. However, the ostentatious formal gardens that sprang up on estates during the Industrial Revolution represented to him, as to Jensen, the "spirit of social display." The sole purpose of these gardens, they felt, was to amuse and heighten the owner's sense of importance. Waugh emphasized the importance of developing an emotional attachment to nature, and often wrote of his sacred reverence for the landscape, as in this piece:

> Of course the student will visit the landscape - no, he will live with it - with an open mind and heart. He will be trying to see what the landscape has to offer, trying to hear what it has to tell. He will look long, quietly, intently at the horizon, or at the distant valley, or at the mountains. And most of all he will consciously seek their spiritual message.[57]

Waugh and Jensen became good friends and in 1926, with Waugh's encouragement, Jensen spoke to the American Society of Landscape Architects, urging them to use native plants and develop "native styles." The "simple tastes of this country" are more appropriate to the manner of life of our people than the imported "formal" gardens, he said. The "soul of a people," he argued, is influenced by the home landscape. Implied in this assessment is an assumption that imperialistic displays of wealth are inherently immoral and will lead to moral decay.

Jensen, like Simonds, developed the idea of the outdoor room, or salon, connected by flowing outdoor spaces. These "rooms" were described by Wilhelm Miller: "Each room contracts at either end, so as to make a sort of natural door, through which you get alluring vistas of the rooms beyond." Similarly, "the borders of these spaces were frequently made up of a series of irregular coves and promontories of shrub and tree masses that provided a sense of mystery, an illusion that there was space hidden behind the massed plantings."[58]

Jensen grouped plants as they would be found in nature, with wetland trees near lagoons and water features, and upland trees on higher ground. He grouped trees, shrubs and ground level species as they would be found in the wild, creating micro-conditions (highly localized soil and climates), that encouraged the health and growth of each plant community.

Jensen was fascinated by time and change, and incorporated them into his work in three ways: the changeability of a physical landscape from zone to zone, the fluid quality of the natural world from day to day and season to season, and the realization that plants grow and change their size and shape over time. He saw a landscape not as a static "snapshot," but as a continually changing and evolving system of relationships.

Considerations of how a landscape would look ten or twenty years from now were taken into account in his designs and although he sometimes tried to emulate in his landscapes a "moment of succession" by planting species to suggest a new successive stage that might be starting up, he never clung to any stage as being more important than any other.

Jensen had some awareness of the potential dangers in using exotic species in landscapes, and warned of future problems associated with them. But I doubt if even he could have imagined that in only a generation the spread of alien species would become the second greatest cause of wildlife habitat destruction and consequent species extinction. Although Jensen might not have shared as keen an awareness of the "bad guys" as today's native landscapers do (maybe they weren't as "bad" then), or of the need to manage native landscapes by emulating natural disturbances such as prairie fires and fluctuating wetland water levels, his strong preference for native plants and their communities marks him as a progenitor of today's natural landscape movement.

Wildlife Habitat

Although wildlife may not have been uppermost in Jensen's mind, all of his designs, and particularly those for schools and neighborhood parks, employed plantings that would attract birds and other wildlife. His designs typically included features such as bird pools, birdhouses and feeding stations.

CHAPTER 11:

Lasting Impacts

The Ideal Section

Jensen was concerned about the automobile and the impact it was already beginning to have, even back in the twenties and thirties, on the American landscape. In 1921 he designed the roadside landscaping for a one and a third mile "ideal section" of the Lincoln Highway, which was intended as a prototype for other U. S. roadways. Conceived as a project to demonstrate the most up-to-date lighting and paving techniques, the organizers had the foresight to employ Jensen to design the roadside landscaping, which was financed by Edsel Ford, despite his mother's animosity toward Jensen.

This roadside "beautification" was controversial. Many engineers, who were more interested in utility than beauty, believed it would add unnecessary expense to the project. But a poll of engineers and landscape architects showed widespread support for the idea, and under Jensen's direction, "natural groupings of native trees and shrubs" were planted to "frame roadside views."

Into this "ideal" road section, Jensen incorporated a large campsite, rest areas, and footpaths in such a way that a pedestrian, though not far from the highway, would have views of trees and shrubbery and the surrounding countryside. Every effort was made to keep these plantings and rights-of-way natural, giving the highway the appearance of a country road. A 1923 press release described the project:

The beautification work, which is under the direction of
Jens Jensen, Landscape Architect of Chicago, is
expected to set a precedent in the handling of roadsides
in America.

Nothing but native plants and shrubs,
indigenous to the country in which the section is
constructed, will be used, but every effort is being made
to develop a harmonious plan which with modifications
can be adapted along Lincoln Highway and other
main roads anywhere between Omaha and New York City.[59]

Unfortunately, strip malls, spreading like invasive exotics, and intense suburban development have all but obliterated the "Ideal Section." But the history of the project serves to illustrate the extent of Jensen's passion for native plants and the preserving of our natural heritage. He often worked on these projects himself, feeling that landscaping was an art that required direct involvement with the soil. Trees figured importantly in these landscapes, and it was said of Jensen by a colleague that he didn't *plant* trees; he *sowed* them.

In the Palisades area of the Mississippi river, Jensen advocated "establishing an "interstate park" by incorporating all the islands, bluffs, and canyons along the river into a giant park and bird preserve."[60] He authored the 1926 Park and Forestry Policy for Illinois, which became the foundation of the policy adopted by the state of Illinois the same year. This policy laid out what we would now call nature-based *highest and best use* criteria for land acquisition for parks. The debt of gratitude owed to Jens Jensen by all who love the natural world is enormous.

Friends of Our Native Landscape

In 1913 Jensen founded *Friends of Our Native Landscape*, a conservation group whose purpose was to collect information about areas of historic and scenic value in Illinois, and promote legislation to protect such areas. They held four meetings each year: First, the "Fireside" meeting in January, then the "Crab Apple Blossom" meeting in May, followed by a "Meeting to the Full Leaf," in June, and finally, in autumn, the "Meeting to the Fallen Leaf." These meeting names give us a clue about Jensen's sense of pageantry, which we'll discuss later. Robert Grese describes the tone of this organization:

> From the beginning, the Friends combined scientific and humanistic approaches to studying and appreciating nature, and promoted the preservation of the nation's heritage as part of an individual's democratic responsibility.[61]

Prominent botanists and educators were among its members, as well as personages of considerable wealth and political clout. The preservation of the Indiana Dunes became its rallying cry and over time the Dunes came to be regarded as the sacred center of the *Friends*. Reminiscent of geologian Thomas Berry who believes it's time to read the scriptures of the natural world, Jensen regarded the Dunes as "the greatest of all books, which "had the potential to satisfy our basic need to know something about mother earth, her great beauty, mysterious life, and never-ending change."

Pageantry

Each of these Friends' meetings took place at a place deemed worthy of being preserved as a park, and the turnout for these meetings was phenomenal. 200 people attended the first meeting. Between ten and twenty thousand people were in attendance four years later when an outdoor pageant was staged to garner support for the *Sand Dunes National Park*. An epic drama portraying the history of the Dunes was performed with a cast of several hundred. Because of a drenching rainfall, the pageant was repeated a week later, this time with fifty thousand people attending.

Jensen's parks often featured a *Players Green*, where public performances could be staged. Under Jensen's direction, some of these plays were staged at night, with only the light of the full moon to illuminate them. Children's pageants were common and Jensen valued them as teaching tools. At Garfield Park's annual *Pageant of the Year and Play Festival*, as many as fourteen hundred people would tell the story of the seasons and dance before audiences of twenty five to thirty thousand. Chicago's West Park Commissioners describe one of these events:

First came girls in bright dresses, carrying flowers - they were the garden flowers. Then came other children as butterflies, bees, humming birds and grasshoppers. All danced and skipped merrily about the green, with the light-heartedness of spring. Liberty and the Thirteen Original States appeared, followed by boys in brown gowns, carrying cherry trees. Here scarecrows were kept busy driving blackbirds away from the fruit. Birds and insects played among the trees.

The Spirit of Peace ushered in Peace Day, while groups of happy beings followed her. Pretty little girls representing wild flowers added to the scene, all dressed in radiant colors. Late summer flowers were blended into the picture while all the birds, flowers and field insects of summer indulged in a revel. These slowly disappeared and only The Last Rose of Summer remained, to drop her petals over a deserted field.

Autumn was introduced by a flock of small girls, dressed as bluebirds. Apple trees, nut trees, harvesters and ghosts danced about the field in turn. Indian Summer was presented by the wrestling of Hiawatha and Mondamin. A band of Indians followed and danced about fires after having given thanks for the harvest. Winter was next, with snowflakes and snow elves. Winter made way for Father Time and the New Year, attended by little girls representing the twelve months. A confusion of snowbirds, snowmen, snowballs, holly and mistletoe romped on.

Snow returned as the dancers departed, only to vanish before the sunshine and wind. Spring came, introduced by Persephone, accompanied by Ceres and her attendants. Arbor Day and St. Patrick's Day entered; April followed with a thunderstorm and showers. A rainbow led to merrymaking around a Maypole.

June, with flowers and butterflies, completed the pageant.[62]

When our grandchildren ask us what people did for entertainment before television and video games, we might tell them about this event, with pangs of nostalgia for a time when people threw themselves into elaborate pageants like this one, almost always outdoors, where the natural world became one of the players.

In 1935 Jensen was commissioned to design the Lincoln Memorial Garden in Springfield, Illinois. "Because many of the species suggested by Jensen were unavailable from nurseries, the school children and garden clubs of Illinois were called on to help collect acorns and other seeds and to gather plants from nature in a grand ceremony performed by local Boy Scouts and Girl Scouts. Other helpers carefully placed hundreds of young saplings by hand . . . volunteers brought in wild plants in their automobiles by the trunkful, and as shade developed, understory plants were added."[63]

Today Lincoln Memorial Park remains pretty much as Jensen intended it, with a mature oak grove grown from acorns collected and planted by Illinois school children. The garden is now used as a regional center for environmental education.

Pageantry was a technique often employed by Jensen to gain popular support for his conservation causes, possibly a reflection of his friendship with Frank Waugh, who as a musician, valued the emotional impact of art and public performance. Keeping people involved with nature requires engaging hearts and souls as well as minds. Jensen knew this to be true.

Another common feature of Jensen's parks was the *council ring*, where people could gather for small outdoor classes, story-telling or performance, or just to hang out together. These also reflected his passion for democracy, for he believed that when people came together, - seated in a circle with everyone on the same level, - democracy was created. His larger parks usually have several of these *council rings* strategically placed to encourage environmental education and conversation.

Reading Robert Grese's book, *Jens Jensen: Maker of Natural Parks and Gardens*, it was these pageants and council rings that most captured my imagination. By using them, Jensen was able to generate massive public support for his conservation efforts. I suspect this is a technique that could be better employed by activists today. Rivers that have been cleaned up, or are on their way to being cleaned up, could be dedicated in this way. Local governments that are pulling together to preserve their natural heritage, could benefit from putting on township-wide pageants. Today we would probably call them something else, like "celebrations" or "dedication ceremonies", but employing the arts and involving school children could generate a unity of spirit for these projects.

Even small events, such as Grese's neighborhood "burn party" can sweep others into a joyful embracing of these positive efforts. Although today there is much more in the world of entertainment competing for peoples' time, we can build on Jensen's intuition and employ pageantry as a means of bringing others into our cause.

Jensen's Legacy

Over eight decades later, echoing Jensen's work, former first lady Lady Bird Johnson and Actress Helen Hayes started an organization that later became known as the *Lady Bird Johnson Wildflower Center* at the University of Texas in Austin. Founded in 1982, the institution is devoted to research and teaching, striving to increase the sustainable use and conservation of native plants and landscapes.

Lady Bird, who once bought several acres of Texas roadside property to save from the bulldozers the native bluebonnets (*Lupinus subcarnosus*) that were blooming there, is often credited with re-awakening the nation to conservation, which had been largely forgotten since the time of Teddy Roosevelt and later, Franklin D. Roosevelt. Among the major legislative initiatives she was influential in getting passed were the Wilderness Act of 1964, the Land and Water Conservation Fund, the Wild and Scenic Rivers Program and many additions to the National Park system, for a total, according to the Lady Bird Johnson Wildflower Center, of 200 laws relevant to the environment.

Today, organizations like the *Lady Bird Johnson Center* are popping up everywhere, as well as a great many small individual initiatives. These efforts, large and small, owe their origins to Jens Jensen. Today's bioregionalists, who are motivating people to find out about the place where they live, the flora and fauna that belong there, and the unique characteristics of their bioregion, are one example. Bioregions are defined not by political boundaries, but by natural features such as mountains, watersheds, waterways, and climate, as well as plants and animals that are native to the region. We can thank Jens Jensen for first recognizing and honoring the Midwestern prairie bioregion as he did. Perhaps he and his contemporaries were the first bioregionalists.

Echoes of Jensen reverberate in this story from the Nature Conservancy: "In 1998 the demand for seedlings in Illinois exceeded the state tree nursery supply by 5.6 million."[64] Just as Jensen had done in Lincoln Memorial Park more than fifty years earlier, the Nature Conservancy turned to boy scouts and girl scouts to gather acorns for their annual "Acorn Roundup" for the reforestation of the Cache River wetlands in southern Illinois. In 1999, with these acorns, the Nature Conservancy established a hardwood tree nursery at its 2,800-acre *Grassy Slough Preserve* in the Cache River wetlands. "The nursery produced enough seedlings - approximately 350,000 - to plant 833 acres of the preserve . . . an important stop for Mississippi flyway waterfowl." [65]

New movements to make cities and suburbs more sustainable are also building on Jensen's work. Jensen predicted that the nation's undoing would stem from polluted and congested cities. He believed there was a better way to live in community, and that communities could be planned to encourage sustainability. As he said, "We have no right to consider ourselves civilized as long as we permit less fortunate residents of our city to live and multiply in unhealthy surroundings that are devoid of beauty and that are a peril to the whole population, and a menace."[66]

City and township planners would do well to review Jensen's work and adopt some of his strategies for greening and humanizing urban landscapes. Even in the twenties, he decried the loss of so many people to the suburbs, where "the average suburban town or village does not present the normal life which is found in a self-sustaining community."[67]   Suburbs are often devoid of character, with their predictable instant landscapes. These "Stepford subdivisions" have the *appearance* of health, with no idea of what true ecological health looks, sounds, or feels like. Our cities are often worse.

Like many who are on the leading edge of today's social change, Jensen called the task of our times that of making the modern city livable. Now, even those of us who live in cities can, thanks to Jensen and his contemporary counterparts, begin to imagine ways of integrating open spaces, homes, and commercial businesses into one sustainable fabric.

For Jensen, conservation was a sacred responsibility, and many of today's homeowners recognize that it starts on our own property and how we choose to be with it. Those of us who are involved in finding new ways of relating with our land can build on the work of Jensen and others like him. This movement is not isolated from the culture as a whole, for we are in the midst of an evolving new paradigm, one that articulates in a deeper way many of the things Jensen intuited. In the same way that the impressionist artists foreshadowed scientific discoveries about the properties of light and relativity, today's natural landscape movement was presaged by Jensen's work.

Jensen's ideas, now fully democratized and spreading across America, yard by yard, are an expression of a new consciousness dawning in the American mind.

CHAPTER 12:

A New Lawn Aesthetic

The study of curves is the study of life itself.
Curves represent the unchained mind full of
mystery and beauty. Straight lines belong to
the militant thought.

Jens Jensen, *Siftings*

A New Kind of Knowledge

Something new is breaking into human consciousness; a new way of thinking, an availability of a previously unsuspected kind of knowledge. Not since the Renaissance has such a sweeping cultural shift taken place. Although we may sense it dimly, we don't see it because we're in it. Ultimately, it will affect every corner of our lives. I believe the lawn wars that are quietly showing up across the United States are an expression of this new knowledge. Despite the conflicts with neighbors and local governments that often arise as a result, a new lawn aesthetic is emerging.

It starts, as Jensen sensed, with a new kind of geometry. Geometry means, literally, "to measure the land." Since the time of the ancient Greeks, humans in what is now the industrialized world have lived by the principles of Euclidian geometry, which measures by distances; angles and lengths, sometimes with curved lines, but usually with straight lines. Not that there's anything wrong with Euclidian geometry. It has allowed humankind to accomplish great things. But it's not the whole story.

Up until recently, we've assumed that the Euclidian way was the only sensible way to look at the world. Oh, yes, there's always been a place for poetry and the other arts, which seem to function along different lines, usually not straight ones. In the 20th century, because the Euclidian view went unquestioned, these "softer" ways of viewing the world were relegated to a secondary role, and were often thought of as amenities or "fluff," having little to do with the "real" world. These Euclidian assumptions have been reflected in our landscaping.

Speaking of the way Euclidian geometry has unconsciously influenced our thinking, science writer John Briggs said, "Traditionally we have used Euclidian shapes, circles, squares, triangles to model figures and landscape. It was a process that tended to generalize and idealize the natural world."[68] Our geometry has influenced the way we design the land as we've attempted to simplify and abstract the natural world according to Euclidian principles. In its most extreme form, we see the creation of instant landscapes that give the impression of health to an increasingly degraded world; trees yanked out of their niches and new trees brought in to pretend they've been there all along; shrubs and perennials whose progenitors were imported from foreign shores; lawns measured and rolled out by the yard like carpeting.

Fractal Geometry

Now new knowledge is putting the Euclidian view in perspective. The new knowledge I'm speaking of is a new kind of geometry, *Fractal* Geometry. Fractal Geometry deals with what mathematician Benoit Mandelbrot calls *dynamical systems* and all the stuff that goes on in the wrinkles and dents of what appear to be smooth, orderly forms. This messy activity exists at microscopic and sub-atomic levels in every seemingly straight and smooth plane and line of every "orderly" system. Fractal geometry reveals a hidden universe of complexity embedded in our reality - one that can open us to the subtlety of the natural world. Could Jens Jensen's rebellion against the geometric formal French garden have been prophetic?

While we've been energetically striving to overcome chaos in the world, fending off the dissipation we've come to expect from the second law of thermodynamics, calling upon our highest creativity to create order and stability, we've overlooked an enchanting world right at our fingertips; one based on the instability and unpredictability that brings a system to a new organizational regime. Although its discovery is new, its effect is not. Incredible beauty lives in the cracks between the worlds of order and chaos. It is the beauty of turbulence.

This turbulent beauty has always resided in the human heart and humans have always found resonance with it in nature: waves crashing upon a rocky shore; storm clouds gathering on the horizon; the pattern of bare branches against the winter sky; wavy lines in the sand on the beach. Aunt Bumps and Jens Jensen were responding to it when they chose randomness over predictability in their landscape designs. People who are creating native landscapes today are responding to it when they go for a tangled look instead of neat rows.

This bizarre new world is performed on a stage where order and chaos intersect. Here, inviting curves called *Strange Attractors* lure old orders into new states of being. Things are transformed here; old stuff is changed completely and new stuff emerges. It's as exciting and unpredictable a world as anyone could possibly imagine. In fact, no one really *did* imagine it until recently, when Benoit Mandelbrot was able to run a simple equation on a computer.

Though the equation itself was simple, it would have taken hundreds of years to calculate its results without computers. For the first time, humans were able to see a visual representation of the world of order at the edge of chaos. Now we know it's there, and it's changing the way we think about everything. Different from Euclidian Geometry, whose elegance was experienced through its predictability, Fractal Geometry is a doorway into the unpredictable world of aesthetics.

Psychiatrist Gerald May has defined aesthetics as a balance, or interaction of the familiar with the novel. This could also be a definition of the world of Fractal Geometry. It might strike the reader as quite a leap from geometry to lawns, but bear with me. We look at a Euclidian lawn, the one described in the introduction to this book. It looks smooth, predictable, and although perhaps somewhat rolling, we kind of know what to expect. If this lawn were in England, you wouldn't even see the ditched fence, appropriately called a "ha-ha", cleverly constructed so that from a distance you don't know it's there.

The vista is comforting. It tells us what we want to know. However, some might find it a boring trivialization of the natural world. Patterns human beings generally find aesthetically pleasing are in dynamic balance. According to John Briggs, "Too much order and it will be like the test bars on a TV screen. Too much noise is like static. You want something in between."[69]

Now look at a fractal or dynamical lawn. It's a riot. But not totally a riot. There are systems of curves - strange attractors, formed by curved garden-edges, tree-branches and plant shapes - inviting you into the unknown, where you might be surprised by beauty. Some places are flat, trimmed, and orderly. But there, right next to them, is a wild place where things tumble over each other in apparent disarray. At first this area looks chaotic. But look closer. The milkweeds (Asclepias) are all gathering together in one area, as if a landscape architect put them there. The grey dogwoods (Cornus foemina) cluster into a copse whose branches end all together in a graceful curve where the branches leave off. Who orchestrated this? Over there, a stand of New Jersey tea (Ceanothus) echoes the curve of the dogwood copse. They punctuate the end of the path, all ending at the same time, all on the same note. Whose baton came down to tell them when to do this? They just did it themselves? Yes, and no.

By not interfering with them, you, the lawn keeper (lawn *beholder* might be a better term), have allowed them to sort themselves out; to find a new order in the chaos they wrassle in. Voila! They have orchestrated themselves. The harmful bugs that might be attracted to the milkweed don't like the dogwood next to them, so they leave the milkweed alone. The milkweed is healthy. The dogwood is healthy too because it has natural defenses against other insects, defenses that that have been developed over thousands of years. The milkweed attracts monarch butterfly caterpillars, who require the milkweed to complete their life cycle. This pleases you so you leave the milkweed alone, which is exactly what the milkweed and the monarchs and the dogwood want.

There's a subtle harmonic convergence going on before your eyes, and you drink it in just because it's interesting and aesthetically pleasing. Things move here. Life lives here. Evening comes. Crickets and frogs and tree toads, who love this place, begin to sing. You eavesdrop as they sing to each other and you pretend they are singing to you. Your heart opens and fills.

A dynamical lawn can be thought of as a lawn where chaos and order interact to create pleasing, harmonic new patterns. Since I've lived with such a lawn for some years now, I've come to call it a contemplative lawn, a lawn that presents an occasion for contemplation. The curving paths through the tall grass and gardens invite my eye around the pond. Long summer evenings find me mesmerized on my deck, pulled by deep shadows and the mystery of understory foliage, dwelling in the profound blue behind the bench, enchanted by the complexity of glittering spikes of water iris; all of it lit by the lowering sun, poured out like glowing honey over the landscape. I've observed guests falling silent too, as they too sink into deep contemplation.

Dynamical Design

Several friends, who were here for a gathering last summer, took a walk around the pond. When they returned to the deck, they admonished me not to do one more "civilized" thing to the property. They "got it." It was the interplay of order and chaos, the familiar and the novel to which they were responding. It felt "natural." Without knowing it, they understood that these two elements were at the moment in pretty good balance and that one more mowed path, clearing, or garden would have been too much, tipping the scale toward order, with disorder and the feeling of naturalness in fast retreat.

On the other hand, they may not have realized that the paths had been mowed, and weeds pulled in the garden beds whose edges I'd redefined to compensate for the lumpy ones that had been scalloped by moles. They weren't aware that three days before, I'd cut with scissors, to a height of about six inches, the six foot tall grasses a couple of feet on either side of the paths, so they wouldn't fall over, obliterating the paths.

Without these efforts, it would have been a mess. Without the mowed clearings, my friends wouldn't have been able to see the tall blue ageratum across the pond, or the bench that invited them to sit and experience the life of the pond. They didn't know that a top-dressing of peat moss had been added to the garden beds, on top of the practical but unsightly straw mulch, to make the soil appear rich and dark, framing and setting off the green plants. Later, the peat moss would be dug into the beds for aeration and water retention. For now, it was cosmetic. A bit of artifice. A bit of order in my chaotic domain. A lot of work.

"So you think I might be one step away from pink plastic flamingos?" I replied, deflecting their heartfelt advice not to get too civilized. But secretly it pleased me to hear them advising against too much order, because I knew they'd experienced exactly what I'd hoped they would - an aesthetic invitation into the intricacies of the natural world. I knew what they said was true, and I knew how hard it would be to restrain myself from the further ordering of this wonderful dynamical system in which I'm blessed to live.

Now that the basic design is laid down, the question of whether I can be satisfied with mere maintenance remains to be seen. The urge to shape one's environment appears to be a basic human need, like food or shelter.

When I started this different approach to landscaping, I, like Jens Jensen, had never heard of fractals or dynamical systems. I hadn't heard of Jens Jensen, for that matter. Yet, the thing that's been created here, partly through my own efforts, and partly through the self-organization of the natural forms that live here, is most assuredly a dynamical system. Are there some design principles here that could be applied to any lawn or property? Let me take a stab at it.

While some of these principles may already be in the landscaper's lexicon, I suspect some of them are new, and they constitute an intuitive response to a new door that has been opened in human consciousness. A place that expresses these fractal principles carries an emotional charge because it's an invitation to a new comprehension, a new world, a new (or perhaps *primordial*) way of being. In the next chapter, we'll look at each of the landscape design principles that may be emerging from Fractal Geometry and see how they might be incorporated into a natural lawn.

CHAPTER 13:

A Fractal Approach

Principles of Fractal Design

A dynamical lawn is typified by its aliveness. Change is the only constant. It's driven by a fundamental (and humbling) unpredictability and uncertainty. Here follow the principles of Fractal Geometry named by John Briggs that might be applied to landscaping: sensitivity to initial conditions, self-similarity, interaction between parts, patterning at various scales, natural processes unfolding over time, iteration, intuitive connections, illumination of ambiguities, interaction of order & chaos, systems of curves (strange attractors), predictable overall form made up of unpredictable details, random/order interaction, amplified feedback transforming into new regimes, a system driven by a fundamental unpredictability and uncertainty.[70]

Let's call their application to landscaping, *Fractal Landscaping Principles*. Suggestions for their application follow:

Sensitivity to Initial Conditions

When native plant nurseryman Bill Schneider enters an "unimproved" landscape, the plant community there is not the first thing he sees. What he sees first is what *used to be* there. His attuned sensitivity asks questions of the lay of the land; is it high and dry or low and wet? Are there wooded areas? Are there open spaces and places in between? Is the soil sandy, loamy, or clay? He looks for rock piles and trees growing in rows, evidence that this land was once farmland. He looks for the tallest tree. If it's an invasive species, he knows humans have been here, disturbing the land, and dragging exotic species behind them. If alien invasives are here, he knows they are now squeezing out whatever native plants might have evolved here before their arrival.

Sara Stein carried mental templates in her head for how certain kinds of areas would look if they were fully restored; Bill Schneider carries a picture of how this land would have looked before European settlement. After he senses the lay of the land, he looks, not for plants, but for plant-*communities*; plants that have grown up in the same neighborhood because conditions encouraged it. In addition, he knows that these plants have encouraged each other, or they probably wouldn't be growing together. If he sees one type of native, he looks around for others that like the same conditions and enjoy the plant's company. Some of these may be "matrix" species - the ones that knit the other ones together. Some may be "indicator" species - the ones that speak of the overall health of an ecosystem, something like a pinkness in the cheek or a twinkle in the eye of an ecosystem.

This is *sensitivity to initial conditions*. This is Frank Waugh, back in the twenties, "living with the landscape with an open mind and heart, trying to see what it has to offer, trying to hear what it has to tell."[71] Discovering the relaxation and trust required to do this is a lesson in humility and an education in how far our minds and hearts have strayed from the natural world. Our own illiteracy in the ways of the natural world is fully exposed and we gain a new respect for the intelligence of non-human species.

Intuitive Connections and Self-similarity

A clearing has mysteriously appeared where I did not plan one. It's attached to one leg of a mowed path that meanders through a small wooded area near where the sump pump empties. My idea for this area was that it would gradually fill up with dense vegetation all on its own, offering cover and nesting places for wildlife, and an aesthetic contrast with other areas that are more open. This path doesn't go anywhere that can't be reached by more convenient paths. I seldom mow it.

From the higher vista of my studio window, it appears that this clearing has created itself around a large rock to one side of the path. The outer curve of one side of this natural clearing follows the arc of the path, and echoes the roundness of the rock. It's pleasing to the eye - a harmonic allegory between the shape of the rock and the outer curve. It reiterates other clearings I've created in other places on the property, in artistic juxtaposition.

Stump-henge, a clearing with tree stumps for seating around a fire pit behind the pole-barn, also has a rock; a very large one, about five feet tall, flat on top, like an altar. It's not in the middle of its clearing where the fire pit is, but off to one side of it. I've mowed a three-foot long path to this rock, and around the "front" of it. Sometimes I put flowers on it. Sometimes I sit on it, watching the sunset across the pond, down the mowed avenue between the pond and Stump-henge. Sometimes my cats sit on it, one at a time, doing the same thing. I call this rock the "Great Rock."

When my friends gathered seven years ago to *warm* my house and property, we concluded the celebration after dark, in Stump-henge. We swept the path around the pond with tall fronds of tansy, then laid the tansy on top of the Great Rock as an offering.

As we sat on the stumps by the firelight and the light of an enormous wax sun-torch Gail had brought, Nancy sang my favorite folk song, arranged by Joseph Canteloube, from *The Songs of the Auvergne*, by while Gisela accompanied her on the recorder. Later, Gisela played a Bach Suite on her cello, as each of us, in honor of the date, (the Fourth of July), launched a candle-raft out onto the pond, each with our "Declaration of Interdependence."

After my friends left, as I went to bed, I saw the candle-rafts, still glowing on the pond. At 3:30 AM, I was awakened by an orange glow that filled the bedroom. I ran to the window and saw the 11 candle-rafts, which should have burned out hours before, still burning. They had quietly floated themselves around the full circumference of the pond and returned almost to their launching place. It was a perfectly mysterious conclusion to a perfectly mysterious evening.

I tell you this story as a tie-in with the story about the self-organized clearing next to the sump discharge. (Should I call this one "Sump-henge?") My human tendency to make mental connections would like me to believe that nature has said, "OK, you like clearings, how's this one?" A clearing with no reason for being is trivial. A clearing with a rock smack in the middle has a raison d'être. The rock is the occasion for the clearing.

There's another reason for this clearing that just now occurred to me, as sometimes happens in the act of writing. That particular rock was one my beloved cat Oobie always sat on when he walked with me around the path network. He would follow along behind me until we came to this rock. Then he'd jump up on it and wait until I noticed he wasn't following any more. I took it as his invitation to walk back and sit with him, to rest, to take time in the middle of our walk and just be. He seemed to think this was a *special* rock. It was the summer that Oobie died, when the circle-clearing around his rock first appeared. Can it be that the natural world has found a way to honor the special relationship Oobie and I enjoyed or to thank Oobie for recognizing the rock's significance?

I've never had to mow this clearing, yet it looks mowed. I've heard of "fairy circles" in Ireland that appear spontaneously in otherwise well-vegetated wooded areas. They're thought to be magical places - gifts to humans from the little people. The child in me who once believed, as a neighbor woman had told me, that fairies could be seen in the moonlight dancing on a board up in the branches of a nearby apple tree, that child, who still lives in me, would like to believe that the little people have decided to re-inhabit my place. I'd like to believe that the fairy circle around Oobie's rock is evidence of an unanticipated resonance, set up by my intention, and perhaps Oobie's intention as well.

Patterning at Various Scales

The roundness of Oobie's rock-circle clearing reflects the roundness of Stump-henge, reflects the roundness of the fire-pit, reflects the roundness of the rocks around it, reflects the roundness of the pond, reflects the roundness of the lily pads, reflects the roundness of the wild ginger leaves. The bowl of the sky is reflected in the bowl of the pond. The vertical lines of the water iris and cattails reflect the vertical lines of the tree trunks. And so on and so on. This kind of metaphor always carries with it a jolt of surprise. Poets call it a "reflectapher", a "juxtaposition of terms that are both self-similar and different, and as a result help open the mind."[72]

Typical of a fractal figure is this repetition at various scales of a pattern. The blob you see on an arm of a fractal spiral turns out to be a miniature version of the spiral arm it's attached to. Zoom in on the blob on that arm and you'll see another spiral arm attached to it, almost exactly like the larger one in every detail.

Jensen used hawthorns and stratified rock to reflect the horizontal lines of the prairie. The curved lines of my paths are like the curved lines of the grasses, the reeds, the cattail leaves. Like a holographic photograph; the whole is contained in every part, and there's something immensely reassuring about that; something healing (wholing); something harmonious. Here I'm talking only about the visual aesthetics of line and shape, but there are other aesthetics and ethics at work here too, relationships we can only barely begin to comprehend. How we as humans fit into this landscape is another question. Do we have a niche here? Is our presence contributing to the health of the whole?

Predictable Overall Form Made Up of Unpredictable Details

"Fractal geometry moves away from quantitative measurement, which values quantifiable features like distances and degrees of angles, and embraces the *qualities* of things - their texture, complexity, and holistic patterning (that is, patterning at various scales)."[73] An example of this might be the pond/lily-pad/ginger-leaf/sky-bowl relationship mentioned earlier. The aesthetic, the idea of *order* in fractal geometry is therefore closer to the ancient aesthetic of the artist than the aesthetic of Euclidian geometry has been.

Natural Processes Unfolding Over Time

Just as Jens Jensen planted with succession in mind, the fractal lawn will change over time. The changes will be noticeable from day to day, from season to season, and from dominance to dominance. At times, one species will dominate; at other times it will retreat and another species will emerge in the tapestry. If no invasive exotics are permitted to take over, this will be a natural process and no species will dominate to the detriment of another. All in this plant community will benefit from each other's company and the community will mature as a natural system does, eventually evolving into a climax community. Stephanie Mills describes a climax plant community and the succession necessary to achieve it:

A climax community maintains conditions - soil texture and nutrients, shade, and biotic richness - that favor its continuation. Barring disturbance, climax communities are very stable through time. Nature being the prankster she is, however, disturbance inevitably occurs, and in the disturbed areas successional processes are set in motion. Different plants are adapted to take advantage of the set of conditions prevalent at the moment, each through its life cycle changing those conditions toward climax.[74]

Zones may experience subtle changes over time as well, as wooded areas creep into open spaces, for example, or with seasonally fluctuating water levels around the edges of a pond. In the spring the water level in my pond is almost the same level as the ground that surrounds it. As the water level goes down over the course of the summer, different plants appear along the pond's edges that would have drowned if the water level had stayed at spring levels. Some, who planted themselves deeper into the pond, need wet feet to feel good. Others need dampness around their roots but dry upper parts. These somehow manage to locate themselves further up the bank.

Some like to be under water in the spring and high and dry during the summer. These are perfectly adapted to the seasonal changes that occur in my pond every year. Those that are not well adapted to these conditions either die and disappear or figure out a way to get themselves or their progeny to a better place. Part of their strategy may be to convince me, by looking wan, to move them. A transition zone is an area where such subtle changes are taking place. These changes are to be expected and are the sign of a healthy, evolving ecosystem.

Iteration and Amplified Feedback Leading to New Regimes

In fractal geometry, Iteration means feedback. Feedback is the mechanism of succession, and of stability within a changing environment. It's how organisms manage change and achieve relative stability. Feedback is amplified through feedback. This can be chaotic, but it is a chaos which, though destabilizing, is moving the entire system to a new regime.

If an ecosystem is favorable to the maturation of a particular plant or species, this constitutes feedback that allows the plant to grow and flourish. In doing so, the plant improves its own growing conditions. This constitutes an amplification of the original positive feedback of favorability. This is how amplification works: the better the feedback, the better the feedback. The movement toward a climax ecosystem and the maintenance of it once it has been achieved is accomplished through feedback feeding into feedback. If there's no feedback or iteration, the plant will fail to thrive and other plants that are better adapted to those particular conditions will move in.

Rene' Dubos has noted the same contrast between French and English landscapes that Jensen did. In Dubos' book, *The Wooing of Earth,* the French use of straight *allées* and their shaping of trees and shrubbery with pruning shears is contrasted with the more natural, "not so Cartesian spirit" of English landscaping. He concludes, as Jensen did, that the way a culture landscapes influences the way it thinks. And, in the manner of feedback, the way a culture thinks influences the way it landscapes. Feedback functions in a similar way in native landscapes as, for example, when native plants cluster together for their own health, and their health, in turn, increases their ability to cluster together.

Fertility is another form of feedback. Through countless iterations in the evolutionary process, toughnesses and tolerances are developed that enhance the health of the plant and its ecosystem.

Euclidian landscapes are often sterile. We don't *want* the plants in them to reproduce. Many plants in these landscapes can't bear seeds or have lost their fragrance through hybridization, discouraging the insects that might have pollinated them. Iteration and feedback, as they function through fertility, are evolutionary mechanisms that allow organisms to adapt to their environs over time. Native landscapes in good balance encourage iteration and feedback.

Interaction of Order & Chaos

Photographer Joe Cantrell believes that "late-model human beings, driven by the forces of science, technology, and economic self-interest, have worked to trivialize the natural order of chaos. We dam the rivers, cut the forests, drill the Arctic. It's an attempt to oversimplify, to obliterate the nuance of nature."[75] The traditional American Lawn is a highly simplified monoculture of non-native grasses. It trivializes the natural order of chaos.

Patterns human beings generally find aesthetically pleasing are a dynamic alliance between order and chaos. Michael Pollan pleads for a middle ground between nature and culture, between wildness (chaos) and Euclidian control (order). The garden, Pollan feels, exemplifies the perfect venue for this blend. The garden is the place where we can learn about nature and practice being in relationship with it. "Americans have a deeply ingrained habit," says Pollan, "of seeing nature and culture as irreconcilably opposed; we automatically assume that whenever one gains, the other must lose."[76] He reminds us that many important things about how we relate to nature cannot be learned in the wild and suggests that the garden is a place where nature and culture can be wedded in a way that is mutually beneficial. He finds the wilderness ethic absolutist in its insistence that you can't have both humans and nature occupying the same space at the same time. He reminds us that the garden is a place with long experience of questions having to do with humans in nature.

Even *wilderness restoration* is a contradiction in terms if you take the fractal model. By not interfering with nature after our presence has so skewed the natural processes that might have taken place without us, we doom an ecosystem to runaway wildness and invasion by exotics. In order to restore an ecosystem to its former succession toward climax, we must *manage* the system. A garden ethic, says Pollan, would be frankly anthropocentric. He tells us that every one of our various metaphors for nature - wilderness, ecosystem, Gaia, resource, wasteland - is already a kind of garden. Even the restorationist is a gardener of sorts, trying to figure out what will help things grow their best. For all we know, humankind may be the very fluctuation that is needed to move the natural regime into a new order.

Suppose our Euclidian lawns became fractal gardens with native plants instead of exotic grasses? Suppose we ask our native landscapes to teach us how to be in the natural world while providing cover and nourishment for our furred and feathered friends. Would that not be a return to the garden from which we were expelled so long ago?

Illumination of Ambiguities

Well, the most obvious ambiguity that's being illuminated by this movement toward native landscaping and wildlife habitat, it seems to me, is the paradox that in order to save it we will have to manage it. Wilderness restoration, as I've said before, is a contradiction in terms. In order to get a wilderness back to anything like its former steady-state climax, we'll have to manage the hell out of it. Paradoxically, when we do that, can it truthfully be said to be wilderness, which implies non-interference by humans?

These ambiguities, while not resolved in the usual sense, are illuminated in the larger picture as mutually dependent. Think of a pointillist painting. The pattern is not discernable at close range, but when you back away from it, a pattern emerges. Back away from an ambiguity and it becomes a whole.

Management and trust constitute the operative paradox here. While we accept the responsibility to manage our natural lawns, we also learn to trust the self-organizing capabilities of the life forms we're working with. They do know what to do if we can leave them alone enough. But leaving them alone too much might doom them to takeover by an invasive exotic, death by wrong soil, or too much sun.

We're also reminded that in art, as in nature, too much perfection makes for an imperfect product, sterile and cold, with the soul sucked out of it. "Irregularity is an important feature of art and an integral part of what makes an artwork beautiful and true."[77] Ken, an engineer, loves butterflies. To attract them, Ken went whole hog. Tore up his Euclidian lawn. Dug up his alien tulips. Killed everything in sight by smothering his whole property with wood chips. Then he filled it up with native plants of every description, leaving paths here and there. The hardest part, Ken said, was overcoming his engineer's impulse to square things off, to neaten things up and straighten meandering lines. His suburban neighbors have been tolerant, - some even curious about what is going on there. Gradually, Ken's perfectionism is melting away and he's so excited about the variety of butterflies that now make regular visits that he no longer thinks in straight lines – at least not in his garden. Who would have guessed that a panoply of butterflies would result from fending off neatness? (Ken did!) Of course, planting what butterflies like might have had something to do with it too.

Systems of Curves (Strange Attractors)

Curves act as strange attractors, inviting you into new experience. Would you like to walk down a path that is straight as far as the eye can see? Or would you prefer a curving path that keeps its secrets until you get around the next bend? Walking a railroad track may be the fastest way to get somewhere, but it probably won't be the most interesting unless there's a train coming. A curve pulls you in, glues you to the landscape, helps you become intimate with it, see it up close.

A "legible landscape" is said to be one you can "read." It makes sense. It has a context, a reason for being where it is. It flows with a certain fluidity. It doesn't jerk you around.

Interaction Between Parts

Native plant communities in their natural state are made up of grasses, forbs, sedges and woody plants, and the more the merrier. Schneider says the important thing is not the individual plants, but how the many diverse plants in an ecosystem work together to create their own community and their own design, and how these communities interact with their situational conditions. It requires a lot of restraint to allow this to happen. Many gardeners who, like me, plant everything three times: twice in the wrong place and once in the right place, will gnash their teeth at this. When you've paid twelve dollars for a plant that doesn't seem happy where it is, of course you will move it, but perhaps now with more comprehension of what it needs, rather than simply for its visual effect.

"Landscapes with the new geometry are a complexity of natural forms. As they work out their relationships - the spatial and shape relationships and the life relationships, there's a sense of each thing being of almost equal significance."[78] Yes, your vigilance is required to keep exotics from taking over, and you certainly will want to move something that you mistakenly put in a dry place to a damp area more suitable to its growing habit. Beyond that, you need to trust this plant community to work things out for itself in the best possible way.

The principles of fractal, or dynamical landscaping are reminiscent of the four characteristics of naturally evolving landscapes that environmental psychologist Rachel Kaplan has articulated: Mystery - space disappearing out of sight; complexity with lots to discover;

legibility - being able to see how you move through the landscape; and coherence balanced with complexity; unity through repeating patterns. Space, light, and shadow play a part too, as any landscaper will tell you. Things growing in nature tend to grow in rivers and drifts, as they will do in your dynamical landscape. These well-known landscaping principles are based on visual effect, which tells you how heavily our species relies on the visual sense. A natural landscape, on the other hand, is more than just visual. Its beauty lies as much in what it does as in how it looks. The complementary integration of fractal principles with these visual principles coincides with the new spaces that are opening up in our brains, bringing a new depth and breadth to our enjoyment of the landscapes that give context to our lives.

PART V:

Lawn Order

CHAPTER 14:

Heritage Garden

"It's a different aesthetic," I said defensively. "It sure is!" came Councilwoman Martha's retort. Martha had called to ask if we intended to cut back the seed-heads that were ripening in our most recent native landscape project. I'd written a grant and gathered the most knowledgeable people I knew, Ruth, Celia, and Rick, (Trish was busy with a similar project elsewhere), to install the third native landscape demonstration in our town. This one, located next to the historic Old Town Hall, we called *Heritage Garden*, to emphasize that the garden, planned in the Euclidian, geometric style typical of the late 1800s, was to be an expression of both our cultural and our natural heritage.

Martha's tone was decidedly hostile. I patiently explained that the grant, approved by the Village Council the previous year, called for the garden's designation as a Backyard Wildlife Habitat, and that meant the seed-heads were to be left over the winter as food for the birds. A week later, we read in the local newspaper that Martha and a couple of new council members had publicly declared *Heritage Garden* to be a "weed patch", saying that somebody should weed-whip it. This, despite our best efforts to educate the Village Council and citizens; despite our conscientious weeding, mulching and tending throughout the summer. It was an arrow to our hearts.

The project had been a labor of love. For months, writing the grant, we'd given thoughtful consideration to how this native landscape might be designed in such a way as to make it acceptable in a downtown setting. Celia, a landscape designer, drew plans showing a paved courtyard with walkways intersecting in the middle. Beds bordered with native evergreen sedge graced the corners, with two larger beds, also bordered by sedge, next to the building and to the south.

Aldo Leopold benches (designed in the 1930's by Aldo Leopold and now utilized as a hallmark of native landscapes), lovingly crafted by the local woodworking club, were installed at the walkway intersection, to invite quiet contemplation and conversation. We loved the switchgrass (Panicum virgatum), behind the benches. Even in the first year, it provided a fluffy wall of protection for the benches. Council members hated it. We had to cut it back.

Blackeyed Susans (Rudbeckia), showy goldenrod (Solidago speciosa) and wild columbine (Aquilegia Canadensis), gave *Heritage Garden* color. Martha thought the goldenrod exacerbated her hay fever. We patiently explained that Goldenrod pollen is not airborne. It blooms at about the same time as ragweed, the real culprit, so it often gets unjustly blamed.

We installed low, decorative fencing, to define the corners of the beds. These antique wrought iron fence-sections have a lovely patina. Some members of the Council thought the boy scouts could paint them. We talked them out of it. Most members of the Village Council could not accept the beauty we'd created in *Heritage Garden*. Yet, over the summer, any time a team member was working there, passersby always stopped to tell us how much they liked the garden. Twice, while swimming at the high school pool, I was cheered by people in swimming classes who were told that our team had installed *Heritage Garden*. Council members called it a weed-patch. Clearly, we were dealing with a cognitive dissonance.

A ton of work went into this project, and into the native landscape stream-buffer we installed the year before. Volunteers had put in over 675 hours on three different workdays to install *Heritage Garden*. The buffer, and a VFW Park planting, installed the year before, required another 34 volunteers and uncounted hours of planning, planting and maintaining. Both the buffer and *Heritage Garden* ran into official opposition.

By Year Three, the opposition to the stream buffer calmed down, as the wonderful variety of forbs began to reach maturity and display their full glory. But the opposition to Heritage Garden, now in its second year, increased. Exacerbated by complaints from a few residents, the cognitive dissonance between the expectation for how a "garden" should look clashed with the "blurry" look of a wildlife habitat.

What have we learned from this opposition? For starters, five lessons:

Lesson #1: Some people don't like tall things in small gardens. Most natives tend to grow taller than cultivars do. Certainly our native showy goldenrod (Solidago speciosa), which typically grows to a height of around four feet, was aware of that rule, attaining a height of six to seven feet the second year. Ditto the sunflowers, (Helianthus annus), which couldn't hold themselves up and insisted on flopping over on top of more disciplined plants. Next year, the third year for Heritage Garden, we'll cut these back before July, in an effort to contain their growth ambitions.

Lesson #2: Some expect to see "specimen" planting, with lots of space around each plant. While this is contrary to what wildlife need for cover and places to raise young, it's more likely to gain human acceptance. We decided to use the "specimen" approach near the "front" of the garden, from which people will view it, and reposition some of the taller "massed" plantings toward the "back" or middle of the garden. We hoped this compromise would gain public acceptance while still maintaining some areas that might be useful to wildlife.

Lesson #4: People like bright colors. In its first year, Heritage Garden was pretty relentlessly yellow relying primarily on goldenrod, blackeyed and browneyed Susan, and helianthus (all yellow) to provide the color, with a little pinkish orange in the spring, provided by the wild columbine. In Year Two, we introduced white culver's root (Veronicastrum virginicum), light purple hairy beardstongue (Penstemon hirsutus), rich pink purple cone flower (Echinacea purpurea), purple blazing star (Liatris spicata), blue New England aster (novae-angliae), and orange butterfly weed (Asclepias tuberose). We paid attention to seasonal succession so that there would be color variety spring, summer, and fall.

Lesson #5 Get signage up early. Nothing gives a native landscape legitimacy like good signage, to explain why a native landscape looks different from a traditional garden. We didn't get ours up till toward the end of Heritage Garden's second summer. We're working on plant Identification as well, hoping to design something weather-worthy that can carry information about the ecological benefits of each plant.

I truly don't know if *Heritage Garden* will ever be accepted by our local self-appointed neatness police. It's our hope that, over time, our Village Council and the few other residents who have complained will get used to this new aesthetic, accept these landscapes for their unique beauty, and come to believe it was their idea. But I wouldn't be at all surprised if, after the five-year commitment specified in the grant, they'll decide to tear it all up and replace it with turfgrass.

Reconciliation

The story of *Heritage Garden* serves to illustrate how deeply embedded in the public psyche are the images fostered by horticultural catalogues. These are the images people carry in their heads of what a public space ought to look like. These same images can be overlaid on private property as well. My property, like *Hertiage Garden*, runs counter to these images. Thanks to tolerant neighbors, I've been able to find a middle ground, one where I hope to invite people in by initially satisfying their expectations, then surprising them with this new, fractal aesthetic I'm hoping to promote.

If you come to my house to visit, expecting to find an enchanted place, you may be disappointed. I suspect that the enchantment may be most available to the one who set out to find it – me. Perhaps through familiarity, I've become the one who is most open to its blandishments. If you expect to be entertained, you'll probably be disappointed. These beauties are subtle. They do not shout. Now, there's a heart-connection between me and this place. Notice, I do not say "my place," because now I feel I belong to the place rather than the other way around.

In the natural world of *here/now*, the war between order and chaos is over. There is instead, an unfolding, an emerging and a diminishing, a coming and a going. At any given moment, the overall appearance is complete, but in its details, like life, it's never complete, always coming, always going.

Other wars are resolved here too: Inner contradictions between mind, body, and spirit; the Cartesian war between mind and matter; the Newtonian split between subject and object; the war between the evolutionary story and the Judeo-Christian creation story. Creation, it turns out, is a continuing process of unfolding emergence, - no less awesome than the Biblical account, which was an appropriate story for its time and no less beautiful a metaphor for how things came to be than the evolutionary story that can today be embraced by all traditions. Rather than overturning or defeating the Biblical story, the evolutionary story fulfills and enlarges it.

Until recently, the Church has reinforced the old alienation through its denial of reality as a continuing process of emergence. In some churches, news of the cessation of hostilities has not yet reached the troops. Science, on the other "side" of this divide, has reinforced the alienation through its failure to recognize consciousness in matter. John Briggs points out that "Descartes and Newton laid a grid over the universe, believing that everything that moves can be measured and specified by sets of coordinates. Scientists have been carefully plotting things ever since."[79] Although the split between science and religion has been profound, they have agreed on one thing: that nature is hostile and must be dominated by Man. Now that is changing.

Looking out of an airplane window, flying low over a suburb during takeoff, I see that grid, laid over what once was an area teeming with life. If we were to zoom in we would see that it still teems with life, but it is life primarily of only one sort: human life. Other exuberances are carefully controlled here.

I look inside myself and see that same grid, dividing up my soul, my body, and my mind, into manageable segments. I walk out into my fractal domain and the grid disappears. The place is whole, or getting there. I am whole, or getting there.

Photographer Lawrence Hudetz speaks of his "inner fractal" by which he means his search for a texture, "a pattern of roughness and tangledness that constitutes his sense of being in the world."[80] He talks about a "quality of being" that needs to show up.

I suggest that underneath this grid, we all have an "inner fractal;" a quality of being that shows up at the intersection of the wild and the civilized. Up until recently, we've thought these two were mutually exclusive and one must defeat the other. Now we know they can be in creative, dynamic tension. Honoring that tension can bring us to a more open way of being in the world. There is no need for war, with an implied winner and loser. This subtle shift can heal many of the alienations we have all inherited from the Modern era. The new cosmological sciences of fractals, chaos, astrophysics and sub-atomic physics, has shown us a nature we can live with.

Landscape painter, Margaret Grimes, believes that "not really looking at nature is what can really kill us as a species."[81]

John Briggs puts it in stark terms:

The question is, shall we inhabit a world shaped (as we have long believed), by lifeless mechanically interacting fragments driven by mechanical laws and awaiting our reassembly and control? Or shall we inhabit a world - the one suggested by fractals and chaos - that is alive, creative, and diversified because its parts are unified, inseparable, and born of an unpredictability ultimately beyond our control?[82]

Can we give up our denial of the truth of life's unpredictability? Can we face our ultimate inability to control our lives? Can our gardens reflect life's reality instead of supporting our denial of its uncertainty?

CHAPTER 15:

A Druid in Downtown Detroit

> The people of the city are easily swept into set rules
> and regulations, and the life of artificiality grows
> abundantly.
>
> Jens Jensen, *Siftings*

An Urban Druid

Years ago I read an article in the *Detroit Free Press* about a man who lived on Boston Boulevard.

Back in the 1920's, Boston Boulevard was in one of Detroit's more dignified neighborhoods. Even today it has resisted the urban decay that is eating the heart out of downtown residential areas in so many cities across the U.S.

In contrast, Boston Boulevard is just that, a broad boulevard with mowed islands in the middle. Large old trees have stood there forever sheltering this urban corridor lovingly, giving it an air of graciousness even though traffic can be heard at all times of the day and night. Lawns are meticulously trimmed, fed, poisoned, watered, and mowed. The lots these grand old houses sit on are only as large as they need to be - no rolling meadows here - and every lot has a house on it.

Standing on the sidewalk beside this boulevard, you know you are in the city. A short walk of no more than a block will bring you to a bus stop, an anomaly in today's Detroit, with its limited public transportation. And yet there's a feeling of order and tranquility in this place. I have heard that in its glory days, Detroit was known as the

Paris of the West. On a street like this one you understand why. And you can understand why the gentleman in question ran into trouble.

As I've mentioned, the man in the article lived on this street. He was written up in *The Detroit Free Press* because of a lawsuit. He had refused to mow his lawn. His neighbors were suing him for creating a public nuisance. Apparently it took them a while to get up the nerve to do this, because by the time the case got to court, quite a lot of growing had taken place where there had previously been lawn in front of the man's house. Trees and shrubs had seeded themselves and the seedlings were becoming trees. The place was beginning to take on the character of a wild place such as one might find out in the country.

Some neighbors called it a jungle, and all of the neighbors were up in arms about the "noxious weeds" and the vermin they believed would be attracted by them. Parents were afraid to let their children use the sidewalk in front of the house, so overgrown it was with Queen Anne's lace and tickseed sunflowers. Brambles and berry bushes prevented one from walking across the property and the mailman feared being attacked by whatever might be lurking in the undergrowth. The house could barely be discerned behind the tangle of greenery. The property was deemed unsightly and a public health menace.

In most cases such as this, that would be the end of the story. The homeowner would be cited for violating a weed ordinance and ordered by the court to "clean the place up" and pay a heavy fine to boot. But this homeowner was ready. He was an attorney. He'd done his homework, and convinced the court that he was a Druid. He was further able to prove that his front yard was his sacred grove. The court ruled that to "clean it up" would have been a violation of his constitutional right to religious freedom. He won his case. Others have not been so lucky.

Ordinances and Noxious Weeds

Almost every local zoning ordinance has a clause or two in it about "noxious weeds." Here is the text of a "notice of violation" that was received by my friends Greg and Robin, when they planted a wildflower meadow on their property:

NOTICE OF VIOLATION OF THE VILLAGE'S
ANTI-BLIGHT ORDINANCE
RE: NOXIOUS WEEDS

Dear Resident/Property Owner,
The Village has an ordinance for noxious weeds and refuse. The Weeds/refuse on your property is in violation of this ordinance. Please perform the necessary maintenance required to keep your property under code. You have until (date) to take care of this matter or the Village shall mow this property and charge you accordingly. Our office will also contact the Police Department to issue you a Civil Infraction Citation.

If you have any questions pertaining to this matter, please contact the village Office.

Sincerely, Village Clerk

A woman in my town was similarly reported by her neighbor. The township supervisor paid her a visit and, seeing the beautiful native plantings there, refused to cite her. "I wasn't about to tell someone she couldn't have a garden," the supervisor said.

While "noxious weeds" are not often defined with any clarity, today they are generally understood to be anything growing where neighbors don't think they should grow. These ordinances have their origins in agriculture and were intended to regulate certain plants that made agriculture difficult. Bindweed, crabgrass, johnsongrass and chickweed, all of them invasive exotic species that were introduced following European colonization, were considered noxious weeds and laws were enacted at the State level in agricultural states to protect crops from them.

Over time, the specificity of these ordinances became blurred, as local governments began passing their own weed ordinances, superseding State laws. Many of these ordinances have made no effort to define a "noxious weed," but instead have tended to classify as "noxious" any herbaceous vegetation taller than an agreed-upon height, usually ten to twelve inches. Funk & Wagnalls Dictionary defines "noxious" as "causing or intending to cause injury to health or morals." Although the intent was to protect property values from the degradation of their neighborhoods by careless neighbors who just let things go, there were, as the dictionary definition indicates, complicated emotional overtones as well. Tinged as the word "noxious" is with morality, an element of character judgment is implied. Add to that the commonly held beliefs about tall vegetation causing hay fever and harboring vermin and it becomes a health issue, justified or not. The term "noxious weeds" carries a complicated mixture of emotion, fears about health, morality, and property values.

In recent years, it's been used more for the intimidation of anyone who deviates from the lawn ethic that in most neighborhoods is a foregone conclusion. The familiar perennials, exotics which, in some cases, are invasive, are usually exempted, excused by their familiarity and their association with "gardens."

These draconian laws are still on the books in many places. Well-meaning ecologically aware people who are experimenting on their property with natural landscaping and native plants have been turned into "criminals" by these outdated laws. One of the most heartbreaking of these stories involves a man in New York State who was fined $50 a day for planting a meadow of black-eyed Susans, coneflowers, bachelor buttons and ox-eye daisies. Because he refused to pay, the fines increased, running up to a total of $30,000. Through appeals court he did get the amount reduced to $500 but neighbors continued to threaten and harass him. They shot birds in his yard and vandalized his meadow. Eventually the man moved away. I'd be surprised if he tried anything like that again.

Some have fared better. An 85 year-old Tulsa woman fought back. When she was threatened with a lawsuit if she didn't cut down her native purple coneflowers, she contacted the local newspapers and soon the story was on the nationwide newswires. The mayor came to her house and apologized, rescinding the citation. Now there is talk of making a movie about her.

Lorrie Otto has a similar story. In the early 1960's, Bayside, Wisconsin officials cut down the fern garden Mrs. Otto had planted so her children might learn about nature. A local ordinance had been interpreted as prohibiting such a planting. She succeeded in getting the ordinance changed and then went on to found a national organization promoting the use of native plants in residential landscapes. Today, *Wild Ones: Native Plants, Natural Landscapes* has over 3,000 household and business members, with 43 chapters nationwide.

Most public officials will not bother a homeowner who is experimenting with wildlife habitat or native plants unless a neighbor complains. But they do complain, more often than not. As I said before, tradition and image run deep and wide, and, though ownership technically stops at the perimeters of one's property, people who own adjoining or nearby property do have a say about what you do on yours.

In an urban or suburban area, the lawn is the unspoken norm, departure from which can bring the law down upon you. I suppose these ordinances were intended to keep the peace by keeping neighbors from wanting to kill each other. If a neighbor allows old cars to rust in his front yard or allows garbage and weeds to accumulate, it's not only unsightly, it does pose a legitimate health hazard. Property that is not tended does look messy and brings property values down.

Myths About Native Plantings

There are some areas of the U.S where poisonous snakes might be an issue. Aside from that possibility, much of the mythology about natural landscapes is simply untrue. Natural landscapes do not harbor vermin, mosquitoes, deer ticks or plants with hay fever-producing pollen. Norway rats don't eat anything in a natural landscape. They like garbage, not native plants. There is nothing in a natural landscape that a rat would find interesting. Our native field mice don't spread disease. They eat grain, not found in native landscapes.

To complete their life cycles mosquitoes require water that has been standing for ten days. If you have old tires lying around, or anything that collects water in shallow pools, you will likely have an abundance of mosquitoes, even if you have the world's most manicured lawn. Birds and predator insects that eat mosquitoes are attracted to natural landscapes. In this way, native plantings can actually *help* control mosquitoes.

In areas where deer regularly visit back yards and Lyme disease is prevalent, it makes sense to exercise caution. Even so, I know of no studies that show an increase in tick-borne diseases in areas with natural landscapes. Moreover, the tasty exotics prevalent in traditional gardens are more likely to invite deer (and deer ticks) into close proximity.

Allergy-producing pollen comes primarily from ragweed, an easily identified native, and bluegrass (Poa pratensis and compressa), non-native species that are very common to most cultivated lawns. Neither ragweed nor bluegrass is found in healthy natural landscapes. The many delightful species of goldenrod, which have wrongly taken the rap for hay fever, are utterly innocent of such charges. Goldenrod pollen, primarily distributed by insects, is not airborne

Fire Insurance

Fire Insurance companies worry about natural landscaping because of a fear of brush fires. Homeowners who do not mow an area around their house can have their fire insurance cancelled without notice, as happened to my friend Wallace. This too, is an anachronism. You can't start a fire in the green leafy materials that comprise a well-tended native landscape. Even prairie grasses, which admittedly are flammable, "can sustain heat for only 20 seconds," according to U. S. Forest Service expert David Seaberg. He testified that "a grass would have to burn within four feet of a house for seven and a half minutes to ignite the wood in it."[83] The likelihood of a fire in a native planting is no greater than the likelihood of a fire in a perennial garden. Yet the natives, because they are unfamiliar, are discriminated against.

Some homeowners consider it a security hazard if a thief or a mugger can hide in the bushes around your house. So, for reasons of security, police recommend not planting a bush or tree, even an exotic species, next to a door or window.

These myths represent some of the unarticulated fears that lie behind the hostility we encountered with *Heritage Garden*. On private property when natural landscaping is installed, these myths are often encountered from neighbors and zoning boards. Many natural landscapers find themselves in the position of having to organize to have existing weed laws rescinded or modified. Before Bonnie Harper Lore put in her natural landscape, she was successful in getting her suburb to change their lawn ordinance that did not allow grasses to be taller than 10 inches. She and another resident appeared at a City Council meeting and gave a workshop about natural landscaping to all of the city planners and lawyers. The ordinance was changed.

Five people in Cook County, Illinois were threatened with lawsuits for planting natural landscapes. They sued to have the Chicago Weed Ordinance declared unconstitutional. Three of the five (now known as the "Chicago Five") had been practicing their natural gardening in cooperation with local government projects. "They noted that the very government that was attempting to prosecute them was rapidly expanding its own natural plantings."[84] The case was dropped when the court was told that "legitimate" landscapers had nothing to fear. The antiquated weed law was not rescinded, but no further prosecutions based on it were initiated, despite, or maybe because of the vagueness of the word "legitimate."

There are many degrees of harshness connected with weed laws. Most common are those, like Chicago's as of 2002, that outlaw any weed in excess a height of 10 inches. Although, in the case of Chicago, this law now appears to be ignored and ineffectual, it can still be invoked at any time. In these laws, because weeds are not defined, a legal case can be made on the basis of the law being unconstitutionally vague. Many weed laws have been struck down in court for this reason.

In some cities, such as Madison, Wisconsin, the homeowner may plant a natural landscape only if he or she files an application to obtain a municipal permit and then gets a majority of the neighbors to approve.

Legal Grounds

Some laws allow natural landscaping if there is a setback along the front and/or perimeters of the lot where herbaceous vegetation may not exceed a certain height. Some of these are flexible enough to accommodate small lots where a 20-foot setback would just about eat up the whole yard.

People who find themselves in the position of having to defend their natural landscape in court can do so, on several grounds. The first is the one invoked by the Druid of Boston Boulevard. There are other circumstances where a religious freedom argument might be plausible, such as Native American and Eastern religions that emphasize a harmonious relationship between nature and humans. The Judeo-Christian establishment is becoming more ecologically conscious as well, and in many churches and temples believers are urged to be stewards of the earth. With the right kind of testimony from the right kind of clergy person, a native landscaper might be able to convince a court that it his or her religious right to refrain from planting a lawn that needs chemical poisons, petroleum-based fertilizers and excessive amounts of water to maintain the appearance of health.

Another argument can be made in defense of landscaping as free expression. Should a homeowner have more right to put up pink plastic flamingos and plywood cutouts of overweight ladies' backsides than you do to plant what you want to plant on your property, as long as it's not poisonous or invasive?

Although most local governments are behind the curve, there are signs that this is changing. In many places, most notably in the Southwest, xeriscaping, or the planting of native low-water-consuming plants, is now the law.

The Northeast Illinois Planning Commission has published an excellent source book for public officials. Now in its second printing, *Natural Landscaping for Public Officials* is available at no cost by writing or calling:

The Northeast Illinois Planning Commission (312) 454-0400
222 S. Riverside Plaza, Suite 1800
Chicago, IL 60606

Included in this publication are sample ordinances that local governments can use as models.

Land Ethic Ordinances

If you plant a lawn that can't percolate storm water and requires poisonous chemicals that stay in the soil for generations and kill beneficial insects; if you use petroleum-based fertilizers that cause the clogging of waterways and the suffocation of marine and amphibian life; if you plant invasive species which deprive wildlife of food and nesting cover, if your turfgrass demands regular mowing with a gas-powered, polluting internal combustion engine, you will not be cited by your local government. Your neighbors will likely praise your sterile lawn and try to imitate it or go it one better.

If you plant native plants, adding wildlife value, nesting and brooding areas, creating deep root-systems to filter stormwater, providing biodiversity and beauty, your neighbors may turn you in to the authorities. You might have to pay a fine or be subjected to governmental mowing. If you burn your prairie without a permit, you can be arrested for arson.

This upside-down ecology is ruining the environment we live in and reducing the number of plant and animal species with whom we share our planet. It all started way back, before we knew any better. *It seemed like a good idea at the time.* But now that we know better, a way for society to accept responsibility for the natural world might be to take Aldo Leopold's Land Ethic as the basis for our local ordinances. "Ecology," Leopold reminds us, "teaches us that no animal - not even man - can be regarded as independent of his environment. Plants, animals, men and soil are a community of interdependent parts, an organism."[85] In Sand County Almanac, Leopold summarized his Land Ethic:

> All ethics so far evolved rest upon a single premise: that the individual is a member of a community of interdependent parts. His instincts prompt him to compete for his place in that community, but his ethics prompt him also to co-operate (perhaps in order that there may be a place to compete for).
>
> The land ethic simply enlarges the boundaries of the community to include soils, waters, plants, and animals, or collectively, the land.
>
> In short, a land ethic changes the role of Homo sapiens from conqueror of the land-community to plain member and citizen of it. It implies respect for his fellow-members and also respect for the community as such.

As legal scholar Bret Rappaport has suggested, it would be hard to find a basis for our local landscaping ordinances as compelling as Leopold's land ethic.

Adventurous homeowners are getting away with more and more as it becomes more and more difficult for most people to distinguish between domestic and "wild" flora in landscapes. Even so, you do have to take your neighbors into account. But you won't have to get a law degree or prove in a court of law that you are a Druid to experiment with an alternative to the traditional America lawn. In the next chapter you'll find more suggestions for forestalling complaints from neighbors.

CHAPTER 16:

What Will the Neighbors Think?

The landscaper must be imbued with an
imaginative mind. If his work is that of a
master, it retains youth and vigor into an
indefinite time unfathomed by man.

Jens Jensen, *Siftings*

Criminal Behavior

Marilyn is tearing up her natural landscape. She is putting in a
turfgrass lawn. This, after an intense court battle lasting over six
years costing her thousands of dollars in fines and legal fees and an
unquantifiable loss of friends and standing in her community. After
all that, why would she just give up like this? The reasons are many
and complicated, some of which we'll never know because she doesn't
want to talk about it. I know that during the same period she also
went through a painful divorce. Whether the divorce had anything
to do with the fight with the neighbors over her natural landscape,
is unknown to me. I know she wants to put those nightmare years
behind her. I know she's trying to sell her house and doubts there will
be very many buyers interested in her unconventional approach to
landscaping. I know she wants to make a new start.

The house is in a typical upwardly mobile middleclass
neighborhood. Marilyn decided to forego the usual lawn in 1990, long
before I ever heard of natural landscaping. Her neighbors thought it

was a terrible idea. Perhaps Marilyn was the victim of her own vision, far ahead of her time.

Marilyn was trying to imagine, through her landscape, what it would be like to live in harmony with nature. Her neighbors found this offensive. Exercising one's imagination, Jamake Highwater reminds us, *is* a political act. It affects not only the imaginer, but those around her as well. Departing from custom will sometimes gain one admiration, but more often than not it will earn the contempt of those you most desire to affect. When people don't yet have a space in their brains for the new idea you are showing through your landscape it can be jarring, and the repercussions can be severe, as Marilyn discovered, and as our native landscape team discovered with *Heritage Garden*. Later, when natural landscapes have become more commonplace, the acceptance will be greater.

Helen's experience was mild compared to Marilyn's, but difficult nevertheless. Helen went to war with her city council. Their weed laws probably dated back to the town's agricultural beginnings, when certain weeds most assuredly were a menace to farming. The weed laws did not distinguish between native plants and the aggressive exotic weeds that did, when farms dominated the area, pose a threat to farming.

Helen installed her natural landscape in 1977 and was cited by her city council a year later. She refused to mow her lawn, as required in the citation, and she was fined. Helen thought it was particularly ironic when she observed the city's maintenance crew conscientiously mowing public property on an Ozone Action day.

In a nearby town, not far from where Helen lived, Joe was cited by his city when he stopped mowing and put in native plantings where his lawn had been. Joe, Helen, and Marilyn - none of these people are "criminals." All are upstanding citizens who were shocked to find they had broken the law. Joe received his citation eleven years ago. Today, Joe is his town's City Naturalist. It's his job to encourage such "criminal" behavior. Helen's town now has a woodland ordinance that is a model for other municipalities looking to protect their natural areas. Things do change.

Monsignor Harrington (not his real name) took it seriously in 1997 when the U. S. Catholic bishops appealed to Catholics to be more environmentally minded. Concerned about the environment, and at the urging of one parishioner who was worried about the effect of runoff from the church lawn on the water quality in the creek nearby, the Monsignor put a stop to the spraying and fertilizing of the lawn at his church. When the dandelions opportunistically moved in and the church lawn turned yellow, parishioners were up arms. How could he do such a thing? To them it seemed he was just letting things go. But he kept patiently explaining the reasons for his decision. Today, his parish has one of the most active environmental groups around, proud of their native plantings and working on water quality issues with a faith-based organization called *River of Life*. Often these small efforts grow into activities that have major environmental impacts.

I've already mentioned Greg and Robin, whose citation appears in Chapter 15. Their citation was especially surprising because they live in a rural area where such things are not ordinarily controlled so tightly. The weed laws where they live made no differentiation between urban, suburban, and rural areas. They did not define noxious weeds, which meant that a noxious weed could be anything a neighbor didn't like. Townships rarely take action unless a neighbor complains. Their neighbor did. Greg and Robin ignored the citation, nobody came and mowed their wildflower meadow, and they never heard anything more about it. Perhaps the township had second thoughts about their ordinance.

Ann and Peter are creating a prairie where their front lawn used to be. Two neighbors in their urban neighborhood complained, but Ann and Peter had laid the groundwork, talking with other neighbors and city officials ahead of time. No action was taken.

Robert Grese, a professor of Landscape Architecture at the University of Michigan's School of Natural Resources, wanted to use his own urban Ann Arbor property as a demonstration of what could be done with native plantings. Like Ann and Peter, he installed a prairie where his front lawn used to be. Knowing his front yard prairie would benefit from burning, he talked to his neighbors ahead of time, so they would understand what he was doing. When it came time for the first burn, after obtaining a permit, he invited his neighbors to a burn party. Now his burns, mentioned in Chapter 6, are biannual events that are considered a neighborhood tradition, celebrated enthusiastically with a street party following the burn. Volunteers are recruited from the college to help with the burn and the local fire department uses it for training purposes.

A Friendship Woods

When Lana started her suburban natural landscape, it never occurred to her to check on her township's weed laws, or that neighbors might be upset by it. She just started, as I did, with a clear boundary edge - a wavy line that divided the native plantings from the semi-circle of lawn she decided to retain. As she worked away, turning leaves into mulch, disappearing large sections of lawn, her neighbors, one by one walked over to see what she was doing.

The people who lived next door and across the street, - people she'd never met in ten years, came to see what was going on. Keeping things more traditional near the property lines, a prairie appeared along the driveway. Cedars were rescued and brought in. Witch hazel was added. The neighbor across the street, who, Lana said, had previously "scalped" her lawn, started to expand her foundation planting beds. Now she mulches her leaves too. Lana's next-door neighbor started a natural planting along the property line, and then proposed that they merge gardens. And so it went. The natural landscape Lana was creating became a catalyst for neighborhood activity. No lawn war here. The friendships that have resulted have been so been so rewarding that Lana has come to call her project "a friendship woods."

Big Canoe

John and Becky moved into my township several years ago from a subdivision in Georgia where no one was allowed to have a lawn. Not that a lawn would have been able to survive there if they had put one in. Located in the Appalachian Mountains, the views in Big Canoe are spectacular. The native azaleas and dogwood that adorn the hillsides there make springtime a cause for celebration. Nothing is level there, and rocks outcrop with surprising sculpted forms. A lawn in a place like this would not only pose a threat to the native plants that abound, it would also be an exercise in futility.

Big Canoe has developed and maintained an environmental ethic since its inception in 1972. Every property owner in Big Canoe must agree to covenants and restrictions that assure "continuing responsibility for environmental quality." These covenants include such things as the prohibition of the removal of any flowering tree, shrub, or evergreen. Removal of any other tree must have prior approval by the property owners association whose responsibility it is to determine what are native trees and shrubs that are protected by the community's covenants and restrictions.

Volunteers from the Big Canoe Garden Club are available for identification of native plants before site preparation begins on a new building project in the community, in order to protect them from damage by the builders.

This approach stands in remarkable contrast to most new housing developments, where all existing vegetation is scalped (nature writer Jonathan Schechter calls this "landscaping"), topsoil is hauled away, and clay is dumped and graded. The property owner must then buy back the topsoil that was hauled away and a lawn is rolled out like carpeting on top of the topsoil.

In Big Canoe, the forest floor is protected by requiring backfilling to be done only by a small machine or by hand, so that the ground surface is not damaged or left covered with clay. All damaged trees must be properly treated, with cuts and scrapes, including cut roots, smoothly shaped and painted with a preservative.

Every homeowner in Big Canoe is given a booklet called "Natural Landscaping and Vista Pruning." It states:

> Landscaping at Big Canoe consists of bridging the man-made house environment with the surrounding natural environment, and is an integral part of the conversion of a house into a home. For the Big Canoe Community, this natural blending should be in keeping with its Appalachian Mountain setting and therefore is quite different in appearance from the beautifully kept lawns and flowing landscape colors which characterize suburban homes. Natural landscaping includes the siting of the house, the use of structural features such as driveways, walks, and retaining walls, and the use of plants to blend these features along with the house into the surrounding natural environment. Large and/ or "character" trees, rock outcroppings, springs and streams, and concentrations of azaleas and other wild flowers and shrubs are protected. Because of the mountain vistas offered by these properties, the view from afar must be considered as well as the view from the street.

Vista pruning is encouraged, where trees are pruned judiciously so as to open the view without damaging the integrity of the tree. This is explained and illustrated in great detail, as is the proper way to excavate and fill so as to protect the forest floor.

An extensive list of acceptable plants is in the homeowner's packet, including plants that are deer-resistant. Although plants on this list are predominately native to the area, some exotics are included if they meet the criteria of thriving in mountain soil and being hardy for the Upper South - Mountain climate, with the exception of the following caveat: "Homeowners frequently have favorite flowers and shrubs which do not blend with the Big Canoe design. Areas not in public view may be used for these favorites." If this were being written today it might also say, "as long as they are not invasive." Berry and seed plants for birds, squirrels and other animals are also included in the list and encouraged. On the back of the Big Canoe brochure is the following statement:

Did you know?

That by careless or hasty decisions, a priceless asset which takes nature a hundred years to produce can be destroyed by a chainsaw in a few minutes

That a tree is powered by solar energy.

That by intercepting most of this energy, trees correspondingly reduce the heat load on shaded homes and other areas.

That a single tree can introduce into the atmosphere from its leaves several hundred gallons of water a day as invisible water vapor.

That by controlling solar heat and humidity, the environment under the tree canopy is naturally air conditioned.

That vegetation can reduce the intensity of noise several fold from nearby areas.

That trees reduce glare by their shade and color. In deep shade, the light intensity can be reduced from 10,000 to 50 footcandles, which is the maximum needed for reading.

That trees do all this work for us - free.

Clearly these people love their trees and intend to keep them. In this community, where lawns are not allowed, their environmental ethic is spelled out:

> Conservation begins with one flower and one person enjoying its undisturbed beauty, and walking past. This is a personal responsibility to be accepted by each property owner, each member of his family and each guest. It cannot be passed to another. To gather wildflowers or carry off a box turtle from along the nature trail, for example, is no different than stopping along a suburban street and picking flowers from the adjoining yards, since these tremendously diverse and fascinating open spaces are the personal property of Big Canoe members.
>
> Property owners and their families expect to enjoy this natural beauty for a long, long time. Paradoxically, the potentially devastating force which can destroy it comes from abuse by the people who would enjoy it. . . Because of our collective ownership, we have a great opportunity to develop for ourselves an ethic such that over the years, we can continue to enjoy these natural areas and at the same time, maintain their environmental quality . . . "
>
> Dr. Robert B. Platt, Big Canoe Ecologist

Gradually, other places like Big Canoe are showing up. Oak Grove and Greys Lake in Illinois are two Midwestern examples. Springfield Township in Michigan, to be discussed in Chapter 18, is another.

CHAPTER 17:

When the Natives Get Restless About the Natives

We can't all live in a place like Big Canoe. Most of us playing around with natural landscaping are pioneers in places where we have no legal or moral authority from our community to do so. Except for our unpleasant experience with *Heritage Garden*, I've been lucky. I live in a sub-rural area where people can mostly do peculiar things with their property and nobody complains much. My nearest neighbors are tolerant people who, even though the unfolding picture across the road probably makes them scratch their heads, they've said nothing.

Except for one kindly neighbor boy who offered to mow my lawn for me, no one seems to have noticed much. I explained to him that I was developing wildlife habitat. The light went on, and a broad smile lit up his face. He then told me stories of how his mother had raised a raccoon.

At first, I admit, it did look messy, but in the first seven years I lived here, a sort of plan began to emerge, with broad sweeping beds of mixed native and non-native plantings. I call this the "stealth" approach: slowly sneaking in the natives before the neighbors catch on. Am I kidding myself? Are those cars that slow down as they go by, sometimes stopping beyond the tall trees where their drivers think I can't see them, - are they slowing and stopping to have a better look? Or are they preparing to report me to the authorities? I'm never quite sure which.

Lois B. Robbins

Others have not been so lucky, as the stories I've shared exemplify. I recently heard about a township that has adopted a new ordinance requiring everyone to mow all their property. Better not try anything enlightened in that place!

Stories like these illustrate what can happen when someone in a city or suburb tries to install a native meadow or leave some areas unmowed. But there are some measures that can be taken to forestall such civic hostility. Here are some things to keep in mind:

First, recognize that you are doing something that most people will not understand, at least not at first. If you hang controversial art in your living room, that's your business and no one will complain. But when you do something to your landscape, it's right out there for all to see. It's not just *your* landscape. Your neighbors have to look at it too. They probably don't yet have a space in their brains for the radical approach you're inviting them to experience. It's best not to be "in your face" with it. Although some may simply regard your eccentric style of landscaping as "shabby-chic" others are much more likely to accept it if they understand why you're doing it. So it's important to get your neighbors on your side any way you can. I know of one homeowner who enlisted the neighbors' help in planning his native plant landscape. Now some of his neighbors are following suit. Even so, as we learned with *Heritage Garden,* your best efforts to educate may fall on deaf ears.

Robert Grese's neighborhood burn parties are another example of how to involve your neighbors. Even if you don't think your neighbors would warm to native landscaping, you might be surprised by the positive response you get when you include them in the planning. Cultivating neighbors while you are "cultivating" your natives is definitely a long-term endeavor, entailing hours of education, handholding, and skill at democratic process, before you even prepare the soil. Lana skipped that part. For Lana, it was easy. She built it and they came. In many neighborhoods, it would take a well-planned course of action, starting with going door-to-door. Most of us wouldn't have the patience or social skills to pull that off. Maybe if councilwoman Martha had been involved in our *Heritage Garden* planning, her response to it might have been different.

The next best approach is not to let the neighbors see what you're doing. Put up a nice tall fence in front of your wild area, or plant dense shrubs. The street frontage of my property is blessed with mature pine trees, which, while they do not completely hide the unmowed areas behind them, at least require some squinting and neck-craning to see them. By the time neighbors realize there's something different going on back there, most of them have gone by and are looking for the next thing to criticize.

Another ploy is to clearly demark wild-looking areas from more domestic ones. When I stopped mowing in front of the house, I decided to keep a small mowed area up next to the house. Although neither of us knew what the other was doing, Lana and I both did the same thing. A curvy diagonal line cuts the front yard in half, separating mowed from unmowed. On my property, this three-foot-wide diagonal line is planted each year with four flats of cosmos. Now that I've discovered natives, I'd prefer to plant this serpentine bed with a native perennial, but I haven't yet discovered one that could do the job I've asked the cosmos to do: stand up taller than everything else and present a wall of continuous nodding color that blooms from late May into October. When it's in bloom, the cosmos grabs the eye, and the fact that everything behind it is unmowed is overlooked. At least that's the idea.

If you're considering just not mowing, you do need to keep a mowed area next to the house to reassure your insurance company that brush fires are not going to burn your house down. They don't seem to think gardens can catch on fire, so gardens are OK. It's tall grass they don't like, and they can cancel your homeowner's insurance if they want to without blinking an eye.

Curb appeal is important too, whether you're trying to sell a house or just trying to live in it. This takes on added significance in urban or suburban areas. Acceptance will be more forthcoming if your natural landscape is aesthetically pleasing by urban/suburban standards.

Joan Iverson Nassauer, a professor at the School of Natural Resources and the Environment at the University of Michigan, has researched the question of how to gain cultural acceptance for more ecologically sensible home landscapes. She stresses the importance of *cues to care*, visual assurances that this property is cared for. Orderly frames, such as mowing, tidy fences and walks, bright flowers, and trimmed, straight edges, she says, can strategically be put around what we tend to see as "messy" ecosystems. By doing this, aesthetic conventions are honored and you are less likely to get crossways to your neighbors and the law.

There's another issue here too. If you're fooling around with natives or wildlife habitat, chances are you're doing it out of zeal. And it probably comes from an idealistic notion that everyone should do the same. This being the case, you might as well admit that you are not only doing this for yourself. You're trying to convince others that they should do it too. This means you're a salesperson as well as a gardener. Therefore, your property, at least whatever parts of it can be seen by neighbors, needs to be as attractive as possible. Any lawn and mowed paths should be kept neat, neat, neat. New native beds will need extra attention as well.

Once your new ecosystem is well established, it will be more legible, more comprehensible, and thus, more acceptable to the neighbors. Weeding will be minimal, as the mature plants will shade out new weed growth.

And here is your best secret weapon: Advertise. "Native Planting" signs are available through *Wild Ones*.[86] Put one out where neighbors can see it. This will give your project some legitimacy and explain why your place looks different. You might also consider getting your property certified as a Backyard Wildlife Habitat with the *National Wildlife Foundation*. This is not difficult to do and for an extra $20 you can get an attractive weatherproof sign stating that your property is a certified Backyard Wildlife Habitat. Passersby might not know what that means, but it looks important and official, so neighbors are less likely to complain. You'll want to be aware of any sign ordinances, but these signs are so small they'll likely pose no problem. They're not much bigger than the ones lawn services stick into turf lawns after spraying them with pesticides, warning children and pets to keep off.

Once your sign is up, don't be surprised to see strangers slowing down as they go by, to study what you've done. Hopefully, some of them will go home and tear up their lawns. Too much to hope for? Probably, but at least a small seed might have been planted in their mind. Who can guess how it might grow?

I was reluctant to call my township and ask for their weed laws. So was Lana. We both knew we wanted to do natural landscaping and believed that by inquiring, we'd be drawing attention to our property, inviting a citation. Although Lana didn't inquire and neither did I until after I'd already installed my natural landscape, It's probably a good idea to find out what your local weed ordinances are. Maybe you can persuade a friend to call for you, so as not to draw attention to what you're doing. In my township the weeds that are prohibited are each named. None of them are natives. A maximum height of 12 inches is required in the township's more urban areas. This might be improved upon by allowing taller growth beyond a certain setback. These setbacks should be flexible, depending on the size of the lot, with smaller lots requiring smaller setbacks.

If your township, subdivision, or municipality doesn't define "weeds," or if there is no setback requirement, and if you're civic minded, you might take it upon yourself, as Bonnie Harper Lore did, to try to get their weed ordinances updated in the light of more recent information. However, you might bear in mind that Bonnie is both a Landscape Architect and the Roadside Vegetation Coordinator for the Federal Highway Administration, so her township officials paid attention to her. Without that kind of credentialized clout, the outcome might not be so pleasant.

Model Ordinances

There are several different regulatory approaches that help mitigate local weed laws as a deterrent to natural landscaping.[87] One of these is the permit approach, which is what they have in Madison, Wisconsin. There, a property owner may apply for approval of a land management plan for a natural lawn, (one where the grasses exceed eight inches in height), with the inspection unit of the department of planning and development. The City provides such property owners with "An Introduction to Naturalized Landscapes: A Guide to Madison's Natural Lawn Ordinance," with sketches showing various approaches to using natural landscaping and tips for getting along with neighbors who have conventional lawns.

Some municipalities that use this type of ordinance require the signatures of adjoining neighbors before issuing a permit. This approach is often augmented with specific exceptions, such as those for native planting, wildlife plantings, erosion control, etc.

A second approach, which I mentioned earlier, is the *setback* ordinance, which permits native vegetation beyond a setback, usually four feet, where vegetation may be no more than a certain height, (not including trees and shrubs). This approach has been outlined in Bret Rappaport's article in the *John Marshall Law Review* (Vol. 26, Summer, 1993).

A third approach is much more comprehensive, and involves the creation of conservation districts and scenic corridor districts. Long Grove, Illinois, a low-density area, was one of the first communities to embrace this approach. Based on the *Natural Heritage Program*, which is available in every state, conservation districts were identified and measures taken to protect them. As in Big Canoe, homeowners whose properties lie adjacent to or within these districts must go through a review process if they wish to make any landscaping improvements.

Wild Ones has a model municipal weed ordinance (Appendix C). An ordinance proposed for Appleton, Wisconsin, "recognizes the fundamental right of every landowner to develop and maintain his landscape in the manner of his choosing, insofar as it is not in a state of neglect, nor presents a hazard to the public health or safety, or to the agricultural environment." Progressively, it acknowledges its citizens' "rights to enjoy and benefit from the variety, beauty, and other values of natural landscaping, including freedom from toxic chemicals . . ." [88]

Urban/Rural Differences

I've come to see that the issue of using natives may be different in rural and urban settings. In urban and suburban areas, the underlying issue is water quality. In rural settings, while water quality is still important, we also have the issues of open space and the conservation of natural areas.

In rural settings the use of natives in home landscapes is perhaps more critical because if it's done on a large scale, it can go a long way toward protecting their unique natural areas and wildlife habitat from invasive exotics that have escaped from peoples' yards, and which are a real threat to the native plant community remnants that are still there. In these settings, using natives in one's landscape not only reduces or eliminates the need for fertilizer and pesticides, it also reduces the exotic genotypes, the bad guys that will be escaping into the wild.

In urban and suburban areas, those remnant pre-settlement areas are likely already gone. Here, pesticide and fertilizer reduction is the primary goal. While natives accomplish that, the impact for water quality will not be as dramatic as it will be if people can be persuaded to embrace a healthy lawn program that discourages the use of fertilizer and pesticides. The chances of that happening are greater than the chances that people will tear up their lawns and convert to all natives, although there are strong indications that many desire to do that.

If You Must Have a Lawn

Turfgrass programs are now being developed that make use of Integrated Pest Management (IPM) to cut down on pesticides and fertilizers and encourage healthy lawns, for those who still require that uninterrupted expanse of flat green. The *Michigan Groundwater Stewardship Project* has developed a set of ecological landscaping principles from which flow "Healthy Lawn" practices.[89] These principles follow:

---

1. Use the *structure* of native plant communities as the basis for public and private landscapes. Non-native (but non-invasive) plants can then be combined with native plants to meet design and horticultural goals.

2. Encourage biodiversity which builds in natural resistance to pests and diseases, and supports ecological stability.

3. Encourage on-site retention of storm water and the use of vegetative filter strips.

4. Minimize the amount of paved surfaces which block infiltration of storm water.

5. Link individual sites together to form ecological corridors. Consider drainage patterns and habitat connections, among other factors.

The "Healthy Lawn" practices that flow from these principles have to do with building fertile soils with organic matter; recycling yard-waste, composting and natural mulching; selecting the right plants for the right places; diversifying vegetation to encourage beneficial insects and pest resistance, providing nutrients and water to sustain healthy plants; using only slow-release fertilizers; and minimizing pesticides by treating only problem areas.

Another approach, though somewhat radical, is finding favor in some ranchland areas. *Goats R Us*, a California-based company offers "environmentally friendly vegetation management" by turning goats loose on your property with a shepherd and a border collie. While its use for lawn-care may be somewhat limited, some property owners of larger acreage may find this strategy practical and beneficial.

A Word About Lawn Mowers

Even property owners who are converting most of their lawns to natives will probably still need lawn mowers. "Nationwide, gasoline push mowers emit: 82,600 tons of hydrocarbons, 2,800 tons of nitrogen oxides, 639,800 tons of carbon monoxide, and 1,348 tons of carbon dioxide into the atmosphere . . .

"By contrast, cordless electric mowers, with emissions calculated at the power plant, emit "eight times less NOx, 3,300 times less hydrocarbons, 5,000 times less carbon dioxide per hour of operation than gasoline engine lawn mowers typically used across the country."[90] My new plug-in cordless Black and Decker mower gives me a couple of hours mowing time for an overnight charge. Fitting into its requirements, I mow the front clearings one day and the back paths and clearings the next. Now that I'm in the rhythm of it, I like it because it keeps me from overdoing. It's quiet too. My neighbors across the street claim they can't tell when I'm mowing unless they see me.

The most environmentally benign mower of all is the reel mower, which was first introduced in 1850. Zero emissions. Those of us old enough to remember laboriously pushing a non-motorized mower are in for a pleasant surprise. Today's improved reel mowers are lightweight and engineered to "cut your grass as easily as pushing a gas-powered mower, even though they come in wider widths than before, up to 20 inches."[91] Some even come with mulching features.

Whether you use a gas-powered mower, a tractor-type lawn-monster, a cordless plug-in electric or a non-polluting reel-type mower, the blade setting should be as high as possible and clippings should be left on the ground. The clippings form a natural mulch and cutting high encourages root-growth while shading out weeds. Surprisingly, it also discourages "thatch", which is the result of unhealthy turf.

Lawn Reduction

Although native landscaping purists wish the lawn would go away entirely, a patch of lawn can enhance a vista and offer a visual foil for garden beds or natural areas. If you're still tenaciously hanging onto some lawn, as I am, you can reduce its size by introducing low-maintenance native plants where you don't want the trouble of maintaining a flower garden. An organization called *Smaller American Lawns Today (SALT)*, recommends that you first decide what areas you absolutely need for turfgrass: a play area for the kids; a place to hang out laundry; mowed paths; meditative clearings; a place to play badminton.

The areas you leave natural should be defined by clear edges. (Remember Nassauer's *cues to care?*) You might want to install edging strips, or find some other way of keeping the ground cover or natives from merging into the lawn in an unkempt blur. A technique I've developed for this is similar to the no sod-busting method for creating new beds. A six-inch strip is left unplanted around the inside edge of the bed. Then overlapping five-inch strips of wet newspapers are laid on top of this strip. On top of that goes a two-to-three-inch deep layer of mulch to cover up the newspapers. Nothing will grow in this strip because nothing will get the light it needs. Over the course of the summer the newspaper rots away, so you'll probably have to do it again next year. But it does keep the chore of pulling weeds to a minimum and your edge keeps its clarity for most of the summer.

You don't have to reduce your lawn all at once. Decide how much lawn you really need, and then start slowly creeping into your lawn area with new or expanded garden beds, a little more each year. This strategy has the added advantage of being another stealth approach. By the time your neighbors realize what you're doing, they may have gotten used to it.

I can envision a time in the future when townships will adopt anti-mowing ordinances and give prizes for the most environmentally friendly property. A neighboring township, not far from where I live, has adopted a *Native Vegetation Project*, to encourage developers and homeowners to preserve the existing native flora and introduce natives into their landscaping. This township-wide effort encompasses every aspect of the community, as we shall see in the next chapter.

PART VI:

The Big Picture

CHAPTER 18:

Hummingbird Ridge

> I believe that every community, be it city, town or village, has within it sufficient intellect for a fine culture fitting for that community.
>
> Jens Jensen, *Siftings*

Hummingbird Ridge

Jim and Naomi are buying a new home in the Hummingbird Ridge subdivision. In their deed is a restriction like the one at Big Canoe that says they may not have a lawn. Their next-door neighbors have the same restriction. Both couples bought their homes based largely on this restriction. They didn't want the work and expense of installing and maintaining a lawn, which can run upwards of 80% more than the cost of maintaining or installing a natural landscape. They like the idea of living in a subdivision and a community where nature is valued and protected.

When they started building, the developer gave them landscaping guidelines, identifying which of 12 habitats their lot contains and what plants would be best suited to their property, a gentle nudge to start them off on the right foot.

Their properties are close to the Long Lake ecosystem complex, a natural wetlands area of about 600 acres, including a prairie fen system. This area has been identified by the Michigan Natural Features Inventory (MNFI) as a reservoir of biological diversity, harboring communities of wildlife and vegetation similar to what was here before

European settlement. The township has designated the Long Lake ecosystem complex for priority protection, where "Special Land Use" rules apply. The Shiawassee River basin is on the southern border of the subdivision's property and one corner of the subdivision is within the priority protection area.

Although there are no wetlands within the forested uplands where Hummingbird Ridge is located, the wetland and fen areas below Hummingbird Ridge are partly recharged by the rain and snow that falls in the ridge's uplands and percolates into the soil. Recognizing that whatever they do on the Hummingbird Ridge upland affects what happens below in the wetlands, the Shiawassee River with which these wetlands are associated, and the human communities downstream, the subdivision's 34-acre commons areas, accessible to all Hummingbird Ridge residents, are protected from development with a conservation easement held by the North Oakland Headwaters Land Conservancy.

The people who live on Hummingbird Ridge are not the only residents here. The area is also the home of a bald eagle, sandhill cranes, and a great blue heron rookery. Thirty-six bird species live or migrate here, as well as many native frogs, toads and blue spotted salamanders, who incubate their young in vernal (springtime) pools. Endangered poweshiek skippers and red-legged spittlebugs have set up housekeeping here as well. A high proportion of native sedges and grasses and seventy-six other native plant species grow here, including white lettuce, bush-clover, and wild lupine, (Lupinus perennis). These give the kind of diversity to the area that wildlife need for food and cover.

An important feature of Hummingbird Ridge is its two storm water retention basins, both surrounded by native plantings to minimize runoff contamination and prevent flooding. The native plants in the filter strips that surround these basins have deep roots that can absorb and purify large amounts of rainwater runoff.

By utilizing cluster housing, sixty three percent of the 54-acre tract being developed as Hummingbird Ridge is preserved in a conservation easement as a commons area. Before starting to build, volunteer rescue crews were brought in to dig and save for replanting the native plants they identified. Builders have disturbed as little vegetation as possible, a concept known as "building within the envelope." All of the properties in Hummingbird Ridge are governed by a master deed, which restricts activities in favor of the natural systems within which the property is embedded.

"Our homes will be literally nestled within the trees," said developer Susan Aulgur in a newspaper interview at the beginning of the project. "We're not going to clear the land for anything but the house itself." She summed up her philosophy: "Development does not have to equal destruction."[92]

Springfield Township guidelines for developments like Hummingbird Ridge, that are near priority protection areas, recognize riparian corridors and blocks of contiguous open space. They include requirements to address water runoff, percolation (the ability of the soil to absorb water), and ground water consumption. Lawn size is to be minimized and landscaping with native plants is encouraged. Precipitation is to be kept on-site as much as possible, especially on ridge tops. Wells must be drilled to a depth below that of the aquifer that supports the fen, and septic systems are to be carefully monitored. Parcels adjacent to the Priority One site are to be managed as wildlife corridors and natural buffers to the adjacent natural communities.

Hummingbird Ridge is one of the first subdivisions to be built since Springfield Township, about an hour north of Detroit, began to participate in the *Shiawassee and Huron Headwaters Project,* through Oakland County Planning and Economic Development Services. Tools have been developed through the project for protecting these and other high-quality natural resources.

For Springfield, it had actually started much earlier, in the late 1980's, when Township Supervisor Collin Walls, was instrumental in the township's setting up a citizen-based land use plan, with site plan review standards designed to protect water quality. In the late '80's, the township began a resource-based planning process, so the preservation of natural areas was already written into their standards.

With a grant from the United States Environmental Protection Agency (USEPA), Oakland County, working with the Michigan Natural Features Inventory (MNFI), identified several valuable natural assets within the township. This, and Collin Walls' progressive land use policies, were already in place in 1995 when a developer went to the county, requesting permission to build in Bridge Valley. Bridge Valley is in one of the MNFI Priority One protection areas where a prairie fen had been found, and where the Clinton River headwaters originate.

Noting the MNFI map, the county sent the developer back to the township. When the developer brought the proposal to the township's Planning Commission, and then to the township Board, Nancy Strole, the township clerk, went into action. She and supervisor Walls realized that despite their best efforts at resource-based planning, there were no ordinances in place to protect such an ecosystem. They met with the developer who agreed to cluster housing and knew that a buffer was needed to protect the fen from upland disturbance.

In 1996, nearly 60 acres in Bridge Valley was put into a conservation easement, and a clustered housing development was approved. Recognizing the important role played by native plants in preserving this important ecosystem, and with the help of MNFI, a list of plants that could not be disturbed was developed and included as part of the agreement. It was all done more or less on a make-it-up-as-you-go-along basis, with many meetings and negotiations back and forth.

It was becoming clear that some kind of proactive process was needed. Supervisor Walls realized that the quantitative data they had was not enough. They needed qualitative data as well. He also realized that natural systems have no respect for political boundaries. Working with the county, a second, larger proposal was written to the USEPA for financial help. The Shiawassee and Huron Headwaters Project was born.

By the time Susan Aulgur brought her proposal for developing Hummingbird Ridge to the Springfield Township Planning Commission, the Shiawassee and Huron Headwaters Project was in place. Coordinated through the county, the project involves six municipalities, five townships, and three conservancies. Its purpose is to assess the natural resources in the area as fully as possible, study and develop tools for their protection, and serve as a model for other townships. Both resource protection and cooperation between municipalities are modeled through the project.

The upland-wetland complex abutting Hummingbird Ridge is part of a larger, 151-acre complex, the birthplace of five rivers. The area, characterized by a globally significant 40-acre prairie fen, is a nearly pristine example of how the landscape appeared prior to European settlement. The fen contains native tamarack, white pine and arborvitae and holds a surviving 22-acre remnant (relict) conifer swamp. The township has two other fens and part of another in pre-settlement condition, 468 acres in all. Without the Michigan Natural Features Inventory and Oakland County Planning and Economic Development Services, these treasures would still be largely unknown.

Natural Features Inventory (NFI)

At about the same time that Springfield Township was beginning its natural resource-based planning process, *The Michigan Natural Features Inventory (MNFI)* was completing a two-year study of the natural areas in Michigan's Oakland County. MNFI, jointly initiated by the County and the Nature Conservancy, is now under the auspices of Michigan State University Extension Service. Other counties across the state and other states across the country are conducting similar studies. The county's entire land surface was systematically surveyed to locate and evaluate all of the remaining tracts of high natural quality and relatively undisturbed native vegetation. This was done in a four-step process:

First, all available natural surveys and plant collections were reviewed. Oakland County owes a debt of gratitude to Marjorie Bingham, a woman who, in the 1940's, as a project of the Cranbrook Science Institute, had conducted and published a major study of Oakland County's vegetation and natural communities.[93] Another source of information was the General Land Office Surveys that had been done in the early 1800's. Intended to chart the country's geography, these surveys also included a wealth of environmental observations and information. More recent surveys that had been conducted for the county's watersheds were consulted as well.

MNFI technicians reviewed aerial photos dating as far back as 1937. With these, they were able to determine where wetlands had been drained or dammed and parts of forests harvested, and to determine where natural communities still exist. This gave them a broad picture of the county's natural areas and the potentials that might still exist in them.

Then they narrowed their research down to the most pristine areas, using reconnaissance flights. During these flights of less than 1000 feet, a few new areas were identified, and then almost half of the potential sites were eliminated from further consideration. A remaining hundred and fourteen sites were identified in the *Shiawassee and Huron Headwaters Project* area, as being potentially high-quality ecosystems.

Of these, funds were available to perform ground-inventories on only eight sites. Remarkably, these ground inventories confirmed the accuracy of the interpretations of the aerial photos.

Ground inventories, which took two years, provided a further winnowing process. Biologists and botanists put on their waders and mucked about through bogs, climbed over wooded knolls and dug in the soil, recording their results. "The presence of sensitive plants was determined, natural quality and disturbances were recorded, species lists were compiled, and soils were checked."[94] Based on this work, a final list of Oakland County's 37 most pristine areas emerged. Hummingbird Ridge abuts one of them.

When the MNFI biologists and botanists went slogging through Springfield's fens and bogs they found native sedges. They found places where white lady's slipper (*Cypripedium reginae*) might grow, and prairie dropseed (Sporobolus heterolepis) and edible valerian (Valeriana edulis). They found verios and red-shouldered hawks and blue-winged warblers. They found blackberries, blueberries, huckleberries, raspberries, gooseberries. They found gray dogwood and witchhazel. (Hamamelis virginiana) They found bottlebrush grass (Hystrix patula) and marsh fleabane, round-lobed hepatica and wild licorice. Their conclusion: this is one of the highest quality ecosystems in Southeast Michigan, with multi-state significance. More recent studies by the Nature Conservancy have confirmed the area as "globally significant."

When township clerk Nancy Strole became aware of the importance of native plants in preserving these valuable resources, she asked herself how the use of native vegetation might be institutionalized. From that question emerged the *Springfield Township Native Vegetation Project* with a USEPA grant to fund it. Lawns were targeted in the grant's problem statement: "Traditional lawns not only cost more to maintain than native landscapes, their maintenance can pollute the environment through use of herbicides and pesticides, can fragment wildlife habitats and corridors, can produce more runoff, and can accelerate the spread of invasive species." Later, she came to call the project the *Native Vegetation Enhancement Program,* to educate and inform residents about the benefits of native plants.

Strole says the biggest obstacle is lack of awareness. With the *Native Vegetation Enhancement Project,* she hopes to change that. "What we have to do," says Strole, "is change peoples' aesthetic. We have to educate them about good and bad plants. We already have a pretty good woodland ordinance, woven into the master plan. MNFI has given us the tools we need to build on that."

The township offices are landscaped with native plantings, - black-eyed Susans (Rudbeckia hirta), big bluestem (Andropogon girardi), coneflowers, and asters (aster novae-angliae), so residents see them when they approach the township offices. "It's also cut way down on maintenance," says Strole. "During the hot summer months, those beds get really dried out. The annuals we used to plant there often required CPR and were a constant concern. Now we just forget about those beds. Except for a few weeds that have to be pulled from time to time, they take care of themselves. It's beautiful and it gives our community a distinctive character."

When you go in the township offices, there are natural landscaping posters and free brochures available to anyone who wants them. When Jim and Naomi bought their new house in Hummingbird Ridge, they were given copies of these brochures, as were all of their neighbors.

An electronic interactive database on a compact disk (CD) called the "Springfield Township Native Vegetation Enhancement Project" has been created and is now also available for free download at the USEPA's website. (See Appendix A, *Resources*.) Listed in this database are detailed descriptions of native plants indigenous to Southeastern Lower Michigan, as well as their benefits, how to use them, where to get them, and how the project fits in with other township initiatives. When the CD became available, Nancy was overwhelmed by the response. Hundreds of people from other townships, and even other states, called to order them.

Springfield Standards

Unlike many local ordinances which discourage, rather than encourage environmentally compatible design, the Springfield Township developed design principles for stormwater management/impervious surface mitigation that encourage or require *Best Management Practices* (structural, vegetative, and managerial) to prevent or reduce degradation of water quality due to storm water runoff. [95] Storm water drainage and erosion control are addressed, utilizing vegetated buffers, swales and natural vegetation. The minimization of impervious surfaces is encouraged. Conditions for the use of wetlands are described in which direct discharge of untreated storm water to a wetland is prohibited, so that wildlife, fish, or other beneficial aquatic organisms and their habitat within the wetland will not be impaired. Site design is addressed, with recommendations for setback relaxation. Drainageways are to be buffered with natural vegetation, and clearing and grading of woodlands and native vegetation is actively discouraged, as it is in Hummingbird Ridge and in Georgia's Big Canoe.

The township's goal is to achieve a balance between reasonable use of the land and the protection of vital natural resources. Construction activity within priority protection areas is prohibited or strictly regulated. Regulated areas are identified with the guidance of a Resource Protection Map that evolved out of the Natural Features Inventory. Wildlife use and habitats are described, and the feeding, watering, cover, nesting, roosting, and perching that can take place there determine an area's "value." Wildlife movement corridors are respected, as are views and vistas for humans. The natural flow of one system into another is honored, even when it crosses township borders. Connections to other systems must be preserved and buffer zones established.

Susan Aulgur, Hummingbird's developer, didn't wait for these standards, which were still being promulgated when she applied to the township for permission to build Hummingbird Ridge. Aulgur wanted to go with the most ideal standards she could imagine. Her firm, Aulgur/Raisin has led the township by not waiting for standards, but instead, imposing their own deed restrictions to reflect concern for the natural context within and near which the subdivision lies. This is one case where the developer is leading the township. Now, following her example, several other subdivisions are being planned in the area. The developers are creating their own deed restrictions to protect the township's natural resources.

For Aulgur, it's not only a love of the natural world that led to these deed restrictions; it's a sound business decision. As in Bridge Valley, the properties in Hummingbird Ridge can be expected to sell for 20-30% more than conventional subdivision properties. Aulgur sees the new overlay district standards as a gift to developers, spelling out the township's expectations, and saving hours of negotiation, redesign and resubmission.

Native plants are the key, for stormwater management, and for preserving natural areas. Native plants have turned out to be Springfield Township's best planning tool.

CHAPTER 19:

Zooming Out

Watching Springfield Township's evolving ecological awareness has convinced me that the best place to start with natural landscaping is with the Big Picture. I and other members of our Native Landscape Team have become frequenters of our county's planning and development offices, watching like vultures as cartographers put the finishing touches on their newest maps of our township, wresting them from the hands of their creators almost before they've left the drawing board. County planners have been key figures in the Springfield story. We call them "the map guys." Without them, our comprehension of natural landscaping would be limited to our own property.

On my kitchen wall is a Native Landscape map of my township. I got it from the map guys. It shows what my township looked like before Europeans got here. I study it almost every day. This was the first of many maps that now wallpaper my house. I want to know what my township looked like before we put our grids on it, because therein lies the land's true potential. This map indicates the underlying structure of the land and its waterways. This green infrastructure still exists, and can flourish again, if we encourage it.

I want to know what that mushy area next to my property is - the area where the peepers sing their hearts out in the springtime. Now I have a map that tells me. It's an inland wet prairie. (No wonder I burn out a sump-pump every eight months!) There are 29 lots for sale in that wet prairie. What will that do to the hydrology? What will it do to the peepers? What did the building of my own house back in the forties do to the hydrology? What was my property like before my pond was dug?

I want to know what a buttonbush willow swamp is, and what plants grow in a bog. Now that I'm getting to know bogs, I'm questioning the wisdom of the organic peat I've been putting on my garden beds. I've started reading the peat bags. They come from Texas and Indiana. They have bogs in Texas? Aren't they worth protecting? Whose bog did that peat come from? What effect is the mining of that bog having on its ecological integrity? Can you see where this leads? To insanity, some might say, or else to a better understanding of the consequences of our actions.

Trish says that since learning about natives and their importance, and the destructiveness of exotic species, she no longer enjoys her garden as she once did. Now she cringes every time she walks past her (invasive) privet (*Ligustrum*) hedge. The myrtle that so accommodatingly fills in between the rocks in her sloping rock garden is now an offense. She wept when surveyors cut down a native pagoda dogwood near her property. Now, when Trish drives past a wide expanse of lawn, she says, "Ugh!" Now she feels queasy with the knowledge that the nice understory shrubs growing in a line next to the high school are invasive non-native autumn olive, probably planted there intentionally by some well-meaning landscaper before anybody knew better. Aldo Leopold named this malady when he said one of the penalties of an ecological education is that one lives alone in a world of wounds.

Back in the '70's I remember reading about a concept for the greening of cities called "remapping;" finding out what was there before the city was built, and beginning to recover those natural resources. Remapping is like med school; learning the diseases in order to cure them; studying the healthy tissue beneath a carbuncle in order to figure out how to energize it.

Now, thanks to my own remapping, I know that part of my property is within an oak-hickory barrens (no wonder there are so many oaks and hickories in my back yard). Some of these hickories, the Kingnuts, are endangered. What other things should be growing in a healthy oak-hickory barrens? I want to know. My Funk & Wagnalls dictionary describes a barrens as a tract of level, scrubby land. I'll bet it's a lot more than that. I've learned that Pennsylvania sedge, (Carex pensylvanica) is a matrix species for Oak-Hickory barrens. Funk & Wagnalls says that a matrix is a womb in which anything originates, takes shape, or is contained. So if this place wants to be an oak-hickory barrens, it most certainly needs Pennsylvania sedge. A matrix species, I now know, is a species that knits an ecosystem together. Without it, the system unravels. Next summer I'll learn to identify Carex pensylvanica and plant some – or find what's already here.

Do the day lilies I planted in a curving row next to the mowed "laundry" area really belong there? Probably not. Is the phragmite growing in my pond-edges going to take over the pond? Probably, unless I put on my Wellies and figure out how to manage them. Native bulrushes would be better. Is there anything in my unmowed-lawn (bluegrass grass gone feral), that wildlife can use? Not much, unless I buy some natives from Bill Schneider, and plant them there.

Suddenly I know that my philosophy of doing nothing is not good enough. I now understand that I've taken on a very big responsibility. Suddenly I know I'll be wrassling with autumn olive, honeysuckle, and phragmite for the rest of my living days. Suddenly I feel very tired. Even if I lived on Hummingbird Ridge or Big Canoe, I would still have the responsibility of vigilance. That's another thing about an ecological education. It binds one irreversibly to *responsibility*, whether one wants it or not.

Common Lawns

Despite the fact that private land ownership is intricately woven into the American Dream, there are many contemporary examples of common ownership of property. The obvious ones are the lands belonging to government facilities and parks. Housing co-ops and co-housing communities offer more examples that are gaining in popularity. Cluster housing is another.

Cluster housing, where part of the land is set aside for open space, as in Hummingbird Ridge, is good news for wildlife because it means they get an unbroken area in which to set up or continue housekeeping and to use for corridors. It's good news for developers, who have less road, pipes and utilities to put in. The open space amenity is a selling-point for potential buyers. It's good news for the residents because they all get to enjoy the wildlife and open space. Instead of three acres, each property owner gets nine, one to live on and eight to share with their neighbors, including the local wildlife. Everybody wins. Neighbors are more accessible to each other but still have the privacy of their own space.

Cluster housing can sometimes be a hard sell. In rural areas it's often perceived as high-density housing. In areas where there appears to be a lot of undeveloped property, the open-space preservation benefits of cluster housing are not valued as they might be in higher density communities where people are feeling the claustrophobia of urban closeness. Most people take these so-called open spaces for granted, not realizing until it's too late that these undeveloped lands are privately owned and can be split for development at any time. When that happens, the so-called open-space is gone.

Many clustered subdivisions have been poorly designed to repeat the cheek-by-jowl living most people want to move away from. But In a well-designed clustered subdivision, views and vistas are optimized and neighbors are buffered from one another so as to maintain maximum privacy in conjunction with proximity.

Cluster housing is not a magic bullet. While recognizing it's a step in the right direction, wildlife biologists say that most wildlife is not crazy about living in such close proximity to humans. If the open spaces preserved in the cluster concept are isolated from other wildlife habitats, the wildlife there is trapped in uncomfortable quarters. Their numbers begin to dwindle.

A nearby township recently hired a new staff planner. Part of the interview process included the challenge to the candidate to show how he or she would preserve open space *without* using cluster housing, while meeting expected population increases. Cluster housing, although very attractive, is only one of a wide spectrum of tools for preserving wildlife habitat and open space.

Many privately owned condos and gated communities have common areas that all residents can enjoy, and have established associations to govern these common areas, as Big Canoe did.[96] Sometimes, as was done in Hummingbird Ridge, the open space is given to a conservancy to manage as a wildlife habitat that can also be enjoyed by humans. As the benefits of natural landscaping become more widely known, more of these communities will utilize it for their common areas.

Some co-housing communities are experimenting with *Permaculture*, an approach to designing human settlements with perennial agricultural systems that mimic the structure and interrelationship found in natural ecological communities. With an emphasis on self-sufficiency, these settlements offer solutions to many of the problems presented by global warming and diminishing petroleum supplies.

Some municipalities are converting parks into wildlife habitats. Fort Collins, Colorado has a ten-acre nature preserve in the heart of downtown on land that used to be a formal park. They employ a full-time wildlife biologist to certify nearby homeowners' backyard wildlife habitats. To receive this certification, homeowners must let nature reclaim their non-native lawns.[97] Long Grove, Illinois, which has no law regulating vegetation height, has a committee that reviews prairie restoration projects within the village.[98]

The state of Illinois has developed citizen-based statewide uniform laws governing planning and zoning statutes, with an eye to protecting open space and natural resources. New Jersey has its *Greenfields* program, which functions like cluster-housing writ large, with large chunks of agricultural land set aside adjacent to areas of intense new development. Conservation easements and nature preserves offer another way of preserving open-space and protecting natural resources. With tools like the *Natural Features Inventory,* more of these kinds of areas will come under protection.

Connections

A further refinement in the protection of open space and high-quality ecosystems, and the wildlife they support, is the concept of corridors. As the fragmentation of open land continues apace, wildlife, whose ranges exceed the boundaries of a protected open space, need ways of getting from one protected space to another. Big picture planners are looking at riparian (river) corridors, pipeline and electrical easements, trailways, greenbelts (green areas around developed areas), and greenways, (nature trails) to find ways of linking up large protected parcels. Often seemingly insignificant hedgerows are rich treasure troves of native genotypes. Enlightened planners are educating homeowners to maintain the treelines and hedgerows between their properties, an idea that Sara Stein promoted passionately in her ground-healing book, *Noah's Garden.* In some places, as in my county, plans that take these things into account are called *Green Infrastructure* plans.

Abandoned railroad beds typically harbor species that haven't been seen elsewhere for years. They offer already-cleared corridors where walking trails can be developed under the auspices of *Rails-to-Trails Consevancy*. Efforts are underway in every state to link up such trails into a nationwide trail network.[99]

One of the most striking examples of this linking-thinking is in New Jersey, where the interstate highway is occasionally spanned with wide, well-vegetated overpasses, designed specifically for wildlife, to protect them from becoming road kill.

This linking up aspect of wildlife protection is a good metaphor for another kind of linking up that is taking place, with amazing partnerships being formed spontaneously between businesses, governments, environmental groups and individual volunteers at all levels. A tremendous amount of creative energy is being released in these synergistic relationships, where things are happening at a breathtaking pace. A reverse NIMBYism (*Not-In-My-Backyard-ism*) is developing, as people who formerly felt isolated in their environmental work are coming together and are starting to say, "I *want* this in my back yard, my township, my county, my state."

Industrial Lawns

Now many industrial parks are incorporating native plantings and natural landscaping into their properties as well. Formerly these properties were designed as "power lawns," with the intention of keeping the world at bay with visual intimidation or, as seen in the ever-more complicated mowing patterns at baseball stadiums, as a competitive exercise. Now industrial parks are being redesigned to not only invite in wildlife by being more environmentally friendly, but to be friendlier to employees and their families as well. Some of these also serve successfully as alternative storm water management systems.

Lakeview Industrial Park in Pleasant Prairie, Wisconsin and Sears Corporate Headquarters in Hoffman Estates, Illinois, are two outstanding examples of this new approach to industrial park landscaping. In Lakeview, nearly 500 acres have been dedicated to a large natural area along the Des Plaines River, resulting in considerable savings to the company. Industry and conservation groups have worked together to preserve this floodplain wetlands, oak savanna, prairie and riparian system. Employees like it too, even bringing their families there on weekends to enjoy the area's natural beauty.[100]

The Sears project has incorporated native plants on their 780-acre property for beauty as well as function, with similar results, as has New Jersey's Ortho-McNeil Pharmaceutical Control. There, the entire campus is a wildflower meadow. Herman Miller, a Grand Rapids office furniture company, has left thirty of its forty acres natural, with three catch basins to filter out phosphorus and settle sediments before stormwater can enter a nearby wetland.

South Burlington, Vermont and the National Audubon Society's Visitor's Center at Corkscrew Swamp in Naples, Florida both have marsh waste-water treatment systems. Pioneered by John Todd's *Living Technologies*, these systems, called *Living Machines*, utilize wetland plants for municipal wastewater purification. Sunlight is incorporated into a managed environment, with a diversity of organisms including bacteria, plants, snails and fish, to break down and digest organic pollutants. Finished water from a *Living Machine* is clean enough for re-use applications such as irrigation or toilet flush water.

The 1,212-acre Ford Rouge industrial complex in Dearborn, Michigan is using native plants and natural landscaping on its campus, which is being completely overhauled under the direction of ecological designer Bill McDonough. With a $2 billion grant from Ford Motor Company's then president, William Clay Ford, (Henry Ford's great grandson), McDonough is redesigning every aspect of the industrial giant, to be more environmentally friendly. McDonough says he's not interested in sustainability if it means maintaining a balance between destruction and regeneration. Instead, he says he's interested in fecundity - regenerative, powerful natural abundance. Under his leadership, the company will measure, in addition to economy, efficiency, and productivity, such things on the grounds as earth worms, insect diversity, depth of topsoil, migratory birds and indigenous fish and water fowl in the Rouge River which runs through the complex.[101] This activity is a welcome expansion of the Rouge River recovery efforts, which began after the formerly toxic river caught fire in the 1960s. Bill McDonough has started something big at Ford's Rouge plant. Nancy Strole and Colin Walls started something big in Springfield Township, and so did developer, Susan Aulgur. And so did the Oakland County map guys Jim Keglovitz and Larry Falardeau, the many conservancies that are looking at the Big Picture, countless task-forces, watershed councils, volunteers and individual property owners. They are all part of a revolution.

The Springfield Township story gives a snapshot of activities in my bioregion. But this is not the only place the revolution is taking place. Every bioregion in the country has a similar story: the people in Oak Grove, Fort Collins and Big Canoe who've given hours of personal time to figure out how to govern themselves in harmony with natural systems; the men and women in suits in the board rooms of the corporations in the Lakeview Industrial Park and Sears and Ford Motor Company, South Burlington, Vermont and the National Audubon Society - all share in a vision and a fervent desire to play a part in the healing of the division between humans and the natural world. None of these efforts alone can do it. It takes all of them all to add up to a miracle. These things don't get much news coverage. But they are bringing into manifestation a new kind of human experience.

CHAPTER 20:

A New Lawn Philosophy

The landscaper belongs to the future. It is he who will
weave the works of man and of the primitive into one
harmonious whole, counteracting the scars made on
mother earth through ignorance. He will oppose the
enslaved thoughts of our machine age by singing
with the freedom of our musicians and our poets of
hills and valleys, of far-reaching plains, of intimate
brooks, and of sea-going streams.

Jens Jensen, *Siftings*

The lawn is intricately woven into the American Dream. It is the
stuff of mythology. How do I know this? I know it by Councilwoman
Martha's reaction to *Heritage Garden*. I know it by the defensiveness I
encounter whenever the subject comes up. Reasons are immediately
brought forth as to why lawn is good. It's soft to walk on barefoot. It's
green. It's cushy. A father can play catch on it with his son. You can
play badminton and croquet on it.

I don't deny these benefits and I wouldn't want to deprive anyone
of their place to play croquet. I like my little patches of lawn - the
ones I've left here and there. You probably like your lawn too. It gives
definition to more complex areas of growth. It gives *cues to care*. But do
we really need "32 million acres of turfgrass across the land?"[102] How
much croquet can we play?

Many observers of the American scene have spoken of a long history
of deteriorating sensibility. Conventional American lawns, repeated

monotonously throughout the landscape, tend to narrow our sensibility, contributing to that deterioration. While reassuringly permanent and predictable, they numb our senses and dull our passions.

We can have perfectly even and green monoculture lawns, if we are willing to pay the price: seventeen billion dollars spent every year on American lawn care,[103] to say nothing of the ecological price of a poisoned environment, degraded water, and diminished wildlife habitat; if we are willing to put 1/3 of all native plant and animal species at risk; if we're willing to heat the biosphere with the CO_2 from our mowers and suffer the climate-change consequences; if we're willing cultivate alien species in our yards and gardens; exotics that offer no food or shelter to wildlife and become aggressive when they escape into the wild, consuming ecological niches formerly occupied by genetically rich native plant communities.

We can have perfect lawns, at least for a while. There's no law against it and there are many laws that support it. But do we really want such lawns? Now that we know what we know, can we continue to be governed by these myths? To move beyond the assumptions and alienations of the Industrial Age, we need a deeper understanding of their origins.

The Promethean Quest

The alienation that typifies the Industrial Age stems from what historian Richard Tarnass calls the "Promethean Quest," which has been to "liberate the human being from the bonds of nature and through human intelligence and will to differentiate and emancipate the human being, to gain control over nature. The quest climaxes," he says, "in modernity, in modern science, where the whole focus of knowledge is prediction and control over a universe seen as utterly unconscious, impersonal, and mechanistic. The universe - the world, nature, animals, plants, and so on - is seen as being utterly without soul, without interiority, without subjectivity."[104]

Ecopsychology

We've been at war, not just with the wildness out there, but also with the wildness in our own being. The wild has been seen as existing somewhere else, beyond the realm of human experience, defined more by its absence than its presence. The fears generated by, or perhaps leading to, the psychological projections involved in this pushing away, this denial of the wild within us, have brought on our war with the natural world.

That we are winning this war is hardly cause for celebration. For with the conquest of nature has come the devastation of all that we depend upon for the sustenance of our souls as well as our bodies. Thoreau recognized this deep connection between the human soul and the natural world when he wrote, "In wildness is the preservation of the world," which appeared on the letterhead of The Wilderness Society. That deep connection has been severed and there is a crying need for its restoration. In both his writings and his talks, Theodore Roszak has gone so far as to suggest that at bottom, *all* psychological problems stem from this alienation. He, too, sees a change in values with the coming environmental revolution, one that derives from a growing appreciation of our dependence on nature.

A free-floating grief permeates our contemporary situation. Little by little our souls are eroded with almost daily disappointments. The field we played in as a child is paved over for a parking lot or developed for housing. The tree we climbed is bulldozed. We can no longer swim in or eat the fish from the lake we knew as children.

Part of our grief comes from a sense of frustration. Powerful forces are at work over which we as individuals feel we have little or no control. Some suggest that what feels to many like our own private grief is not just ours alone, but as Tarnass puts it, "Perhaps the whole planet is in some sense going through a very powerful transformative crisis . . ."[105]

Although many ecological problems have arisen in its wake, the *Promethean Quest* has brought us many benefits, not the least of which has been, for Americans at least, freedom from political tyranny. But there are other tyrannies too, that have emerged in the wake of the *Promethean Quest* – subtle myths by which we live. The American lawn is one of them.

Moving On

To end the thrall of the Industrial Age, a new vision is needed, a vision that brings freedom from many of these old patterns and outworn myths. It is a vision that shows us a way to move on, bringing with us many of the benefits of the industrial Age, but incorporating them into a more ecologically benign way of doing things, one that seeks to *emulate* natural processes instead of short-circuiting them.

There are many signs that such a new vision is emerging. It is reflected in many of the impulses now present in the culture. Two manifestations of these impulses that can be noted are a new experience of the universe as *saturated with meaning*, and notions of a participatory relationship between humans and the natural world. These impulses are manifesting in philosophy, science, business, education, and literature. They are everywhere.

Healing

When Rene' Dubos was writing *The Wooing of Earth* in the late '70's, he already was already aware of a changing sensibility. The image of man as conqueror, he said, now tends to be replaced by the image of man as the seeker of a *modus vivendi* with, "the total physical and biological environment." He goes on to name the ultimate ideal as "an intimate communion with the cosmos."[106] The universe we're beginning to experience in a new and powerful way is not an existentially hostile or indifferent one, as Thomas Berry reminds us in his book, *Dream of the Earth*, but a universe enlivened by participation, communion, individuation, and an inner radiance that throbs at the heart of every material thing. In this new perception lies healing. It is both new and old.

Twenty five hundred years ago, Hippocrates recognized it when he wrote in *Airs, Water, Places*: "To grasp the disorders in any subject we must study carefully the environment of the disorder: the kind of water; the winds, humidity, temperatures, the food and plants; the time of day; the seasons. Treatment of the inner requires attention to the outer"[107]

Most of us can recall having been healed by a tree or a place. For Thomas Berry it was a field of lilies. My daughter remembers an apple orchard in full bloom that "happened" to her on her way home from school when she was ten. For me, growing up, it was a cornfield, 15 minutes by bike from my home. Today it's my back yard. The ways it nourishes my spirit are myriad. At this moment I'm looking at three deer across the pond. Despite their appetite for hostas, the magnificence of these creatures never fails to bump me back to a more fundamental heart-space. Whatever activity I'm engaged in comes to a halt as I behold them for as long as they're willing to stay. Gratitude for the gift of their presence fills my heart every time.

Evidence of Change

Although the juggernaut of the Promethean Quest appears invincible, there is evidence that a shift in thinking has begun to take place. According to a 2002 USEPA survey, 79 percent of Americans support sustainability. Today that percentage is undoubtedly higher. Even though species continue to go extinct at an alarming rate, several species have been removed from the endangered species list. The California condor, the gray wolf, and the peregrine falcon have made remarkable comebacks, largely due to human diligence. Our national symbol, the bald eagle, is returning to many habitats from which it had disappeared. In the 1960's there were only 500 known nesting pairs. In the 1990's, 5,000 nesting pairs were counted.[108]

There are other indications of progress toward a cleaner environment. "The nation's air is cleaner, its water purer. There is more protected open space in national parks . . . In 1999, for the first time since record-keeping began in the mid-'50's, Los Angeles did not record one ozone reading high enough to trigger a smog alert. Nationwide, emissions of all but one of the six major air pollutants tracked by the EPA since the 1970 Clean Air Act was enacted have declined."[109] The Canadian government has proposed banning all pesticides. Two-thirds of U.S. waters are safe for fishing and swimming, in contrast to only one third before the Clean Water Act took effect. Rivers no longer catch fire.

While we can celebrate these victories, we dare not be lulled into complacency. Although news like this may signal the beginnings of a shift from the exploitative Promethean mentality of the past, there is still enough bad news to make us aware that environmental degradation will be a major fact of life for generations to come. Global warming and climate change head the list.

The Great Lakes, holding 20 percent of the world's fresh water, are in peril, According to Tom Huntley, chairman of the Great Lakes Commission. "There's a very real concern that the combination of stresses they [the Great Lakes] are facing could push them beyond a 'tipping point' where we could see massive and potentially irreversible damages to the Great Lakes ecosystem." But things *are* beginning to change, and as the limitations of Newtonian/Cartesian science are more and more widely recognized, it is contemporary science that is leading this transformation.

Geophilia and Empowerment

Biologist E. O. Wilson suggests that there are already some concepts, built into the American psyche that can be joined with large amounts of scientific data to bring about the needed change in consciousness. One of these is the love of the land, or *geophilia*. Political leaders are well advised, Wilson says, to value the heritage which comes to us from the natural world, - the living things that have adapted themselves so well to the unique conditions on this continent and were here long before we were. Those in power have a sacred trust to protect them.

The second concept is that of empowerment. It's woven into our Constitution. We here in the United States hold this idea as one of the cornerstones of democracy. We might extend this principle to mean, as Wilson suggests, not just the empowerment of humans, but the empowerment of the flora and fauna as well. Some natural areas, when thought of in this way, remnants that are still rich with biodiversity - are the equivalent of Independence Hall and the Gettysburg Address for America, Wilson says. They need to be defended as vigorously as we would defend these hallowed historical institutions.

"Every native species, however humble in appearance by contemporary standards," Wilson says, "has its place in the nation's heritage. It is a masterpiece of evolution, an ancient, multifaceted entity that still shares the land with us. Each species in turn will someday be appreciated as we now appreciate the bison and redwood, understood and protected by aficionados who understand and protect it. They will ask, 'Why did we let others like it go extinct?' Future generations will know that with a relatively small amount of effort, we could have saved virtually all of the biota."[110]

The struggle to redefine our place in the world is calling forth an enormous outpouring of creative energy. This generous expenditure is occurring through individual efforts as well as in the Big Picture.

Ken Druse writes that if even a fraction of America's 38 million gardeners turned a quarter of their landscape into a [natural landscape], there would be a measurable impact. If every gardener gave just one tenth of an acre back, he says, the instant net gain would be 3.8 million acres of native plants. A national movement of this kind is something even Jens Jensen didn't dare to hope for. (He probably never imagined that turfgrass would one day carpet America coast-to-coast either!)

If each of us did as Druse suggests, a change in consciousness would take place. Our connection to wildness in our everyday lives would deepen and our addictions to harmful substances, both environmental and internal, would lessen.

The real challenge of making peace begins with our own property. This is where healing begins - the healing of the split with the natural world and our own nature as well. We can feel powerless or we can, as individuals, in our own little corner of the world, in our own daily lives, take a stand for the natural world. The natural lawn, creeping across the country yard by yard, township by township, county by county, gives us a way to do this. It shows us how to foster a deeper connection to wildness in our daily lives. As we allow some wildness into our yards, a safe and energizing wildness rises in our souls as well. Jens Jensen experienced this safe wildness in the middle of a talk he was giving:

My eyes shot across the audience into an open glade in the woodlands where the brilliancy of the goldenrod in the path of the sun's afterglow gave to me an illumination worth a million operas, and I silently wished that those about me might have seen and felt this spiritual message from their native soil.[111]

Place

I used to worry about the rain forest. I still do, but now I worry also about my own back yard, and my own township. I worry about the destruction that will take place unless we find ways to protect the natural areas that are still here, from inadequately planned development and alien species.

Natural landscaping teaches double vision. Like the sea chantey about the one-eyed cook with her "one eye on the pot and t'other up the chimney," the natural landscaper has one eye on the Big Picture maps and the other on the specific plant and animal communities that evolved here, *in this place*. These are localized concerns with global ramifications. They make urgent the need to know what native plants will thrive here because they've evolved in this place.

There's a favorite motto of natural landscapers: "If nothing moves in your landscape it's not alive." That's the thing I notice most about this place where I am. It's alive. The birds, the crickets, the frogs, the woodpecker's drumming - these sounds fill the house when the windows are open, reminding me that I'm not alone in the universe.

CHAPTER 21:

Frog Pond

This morning I mowed two frogs - one of them a threatened Northern Leopard frog. It doesn't surprise me to learn they're on the *threatened* list because they're so oblivious to mowers. I tried to warn them, stomping through the grass before mowing there. It's been so long since I've mowed this path, the frogs are not sure where the tall grass starts and the short, mowed, grass ends. Neither am I.

They do know they're safer in the tall grass, if they can figure out which is which, for that is always the direction in which they hop when I let them know I'm coming - an evolutionary adaptation to the American Lawn, no doubt. I felt bad about the two I mowed. I tried to console myself with the rationalization that these two losses will probably not be crucial to the frog population in general, at least not in this pond.

The frogs own this pond. If I surprise them by approaching by a seldom-used path, I usually stop counting splashes and start laughing at about 15. There are many kinds. There are the ones that are green all over and the ones that are brilliant green from the waist up and muddy brown from the waist down. I found one of them this morning in my compost bin - a big one. I wondered what she was doing so far from her pond. I asked her, but she just sat there, blinking at me, as if to ask what I was doing so far from my fireplace.

Then there are the pickerel frogs, like the green Northern Leopards, only brown with rectangular spots. They're everywhere: down near the dock, and on the far path - the high one where nothing will grow except thistle and horsetail. The biggest ones hang out at the east end of the pond, protected by cattails and phragmite. When they sense me coming, they plunge in, and then circle back to watch me with half-submerged eyes.

It's a frog pond all right, but it's also a turtle pond and a muskrat pond, and a heron pond, and for a few days last winter it was a mink or an otter pond, I couldn't be sure which. It used to be a gold fish pond before the heron got them all.

One thing I'm learning about this place is that what you see is never the thing you were hoping to see. Go to the pond expecting to see frogs and they'll all be on vacation, but turtles will tumble off their log like synchronized divers. Put a salt lick out for the deer and it will slowly dwindle away from the rain. When it's gone, the deer show up.

This morning, in addition to the two frogs I mowed, I saw a baby garter snake, a woodchuck, and a heron, none of which I was expecting (the mower does kind of stir things up). The heron appeared overhead while I was mowing the far path around the pond. As soon as I saw him, I turned the mower off and stood motionless, hoping he wouldn't notice me. He circled the pond twice, assured himself that the frogs were not on vacation, and promised to return at 5:00 AM when he knew I'd be fast asleep.

Heading back toward the house, I saw my two cats bounding lickety-brindle, with tails puffed out like chimney brushes, around the other side of the pond. Something had scared the bejeebers out of them. Then I saw eight large ducklings and their fierce mother, waddling toward the pond for their morning swim. In some secret place, this mother duck had raised these eight fluff balls, safe from two predatory cats, until they were big enough to give the cats a run for their money!

Now I'm waiting for hummingbirds. The literature says they must replenish their sugar supply every few minutes to stay alive. If that is so, they must have gone into suspended animation or found some other sugar source besides the feeders, for I've been here, very quiet, for at least 45 minutes. The last time the hummingbirds came, they chirped, in frustration, I imagined, because their perches got chewed off by raccoons or squirrels, (I spread the blame equally between the two).

Now the sun is in its last mellow glory between the tree trunks. The shadows are long, the green behind the meditation bench luminous. Gradually, as this sacred moment lengthens, my being fills up with gratitude. What more could I ever want? The ecstasy I feel would be excruciating if it went on much longer.

But the cool evening breeze announces its ending. The mosquitoes, who are not perfectly controlled in my imperfect natural landscape, know this. With the arrival of dusk, they have permission to come into my territory. It's time to move indoors.

CHAPTER 22:

Conclusion: A Green Baby

A More Fundamental Grasp

It may be true, as author, lecturer and choreographer Jamake Highwater has noted, that there is something in us that wants and needs superficiality. But, he reminds us, there is also something deeper in our hearts - a yearning for a more fundamental grasp of experience.

The green baby on this book's cover is a metaphor for the natural lawn; an opportunity for that more fundamental grasp of experience of which Highwater speaks. The consciousness it expresses is new, which is why a green baby seems an appropriate metaphor for it. This newness acknowledges the past but yearns for a more participatory relationship between humans and the natural world - one that values wildness and its diversity for its own sake.

Why is biodiversity important? Our lives depend on it. Our spirits require it. Animals in the wild and our companion animals as well, remind us that our own perspective is only one among many. With the massive extinctions we are causing, we realize that we are losing these other perspectives. We are emotionally nourished by them. They enrich our lives and teach us things we might not otherwise learn. They are woven into our stories, our sense of beauty, and our capacity for delight.

That said, we must also admit to their *intrinsic* value, apart from what they do for us. They do what they do, not to please us or excite our imagination, but because they are driven by their own desires. A sensitivity to otherness challenges us to know that the eagle soars for its own purposes; the trout has its own motivations for leaping.

The concern with animal rights is emblematic of a profound shift taking place in American culture. Perhaps less altruistically, our relationship with animals is also an issue of the robustness of our own souls. By responding to the otherness we find in animals, we are answering the evolutionary call to recognize that we are all caught together in this web of life.

Inner Change

Natural landscaping changes you in profound ways. Many of the ecological concepts I've been digesting intellectually have taken on new meaning. Now a garden is no longer beautiful to me on its visual merits alone. Its true beauty lies in its relationships - in the patterns and processes of the living things there. Now I'm beginning to develop another layer in my mind on top of landscaping principles such as form, leaf texture, color, etc. This new layer asks how a particular landscape design will contribute to the wellbeing of wildlife.

Nature becomes a verb. Its beauty and vitality lies in what it does, rather than how it looks. In some ways it's like learning how to draw - you never see the world in quite the same way again. Once fully acquainted with a native spicebush (Lindera benzoin) you will see not just the subtle beauty of its form and texture. You will see not only the spicebush, but also the tiger swallowtail butterflies who require it for their life cycle, even if none are present at the moment. You'll see the other plants around the spicebush, who grow with them in community. You'll see the birds who eat the insects these plants attract, even if the birds have gone south for the winter. You'll understand how these interdependencies ultimately affect humans with the realization that ultimately, all of our food is fertilized by animals. You'll see a whole interacting web of relationships. And seeing it, you'll be in relationship too. You'll not only be seeing it, you'll be hearing it deeply.

As we develop a new sensitivity, a new listening to what our property wants to be, an unexpected beauty emerges. A listening that goes this deep requires an attitude of caring, best expressed in the Latin word, *caritas* which is sometimes translated as "charity" – an open-hearted receptiveness and reciprocity that can be thought of as love in action. Miracles emerge in its presence. Ecological balance, it seems, has aesthetic and spiritual dimensions.

Having cultivated this deep listening, you'll be able to listen more deeply to other people as well. Enchantment will return to the world, slowly at first, but sometimes in startling ways, as I experienced with six young deer who sped around my pond in playful abandon, and a killdeer who once showed me where not to mow.

A Radical Boundary Dissolves

The fact that so many people are now awakening from the Cartesian dream, which drew such a radical boundary between us humans as "subject" and the natural world as "object," tells me that it might not be too late. We are coming to realize that although now highly autonomous and differentiated, we are yet held lovingly in a universe that is juicy with meaning. We are beginning to feel in our bones, some of us, that creativity originates not with the human, but constitutes the very ocean in which our lives swim. We dwell within Anima Mundi, or World Soul. It throbs within us. Many contemporary writers are articulating a new sensibility, as Peter Russell does when he states, "Whatever the creature, the essence of consciousness remains the same. It is the essence of being aware, the light behind all experience. Seeing this, seeing that the consciousness within ourselves is the same consciousness that lies within all sentient beings is the basis of universal love, a love for all creation."[112]

With this new way of being comes a more secure place for ourselves in the scheme of things. Out of that security grows a wedding of knowing and acting. From it flows gratitude, and I cannot think of a more perfect way to experience and express gratitude than through the practice of natural landscaping.

Aldo Leopold's *land ethic* held that a thing is right when it tends to preserve the stability and the integrity of a biotic community; wrong when it tends otherwise. Leopold believed that the Land Ethic would never succeed unless practiced by private citizens. He said, "A land ethic . . . reflects the existence of an ecological conscience and this in turn reflects a conviction of individual responsibility for the health of the land."[113]

A Green Baby

On my windowsill sits a tiny green baby, no bigger than the top part of my thumb. Its arms are outstretched. On Its face is a look of trust and eager expectation. It's waiting to be picked up, held lovingly, cuddled, comforted. It came to me by magic.

Suzanne and Mary Ann have a wildfowl sanctuary down the road, about a half-mile from where I live. Licensed as wildlife rehabilitators, they've fought with the local planning commission for permission to keep a travel trailer on their eight-acre sanctuary. They believed the trailer was needed to deter hunters, who were cutting through the fence and killing the birds the women are trying to protect.

When I read about it in the local papers, I wrote letters to the editor and the Planning Commission, in support of Suzanne and Mary Ann's cause. Their gratitude has caused them to shower me with sweet pastries, culled from an unending supply of day-old bakery products they've been given for the birds. One of these delectables was a King Cake - a glorified coffee cake coated with generous globs of purple, gold and green frosting topped by sugar-glitter.

The King Cake, the label on the box explains, is a Mardi Gras tradition, and Louisianans might not know that Lent is about to begin without King Cakes showing up everywhere. Every King Cake has a baby, like the one on my windowsill, nestled into the frosting. My baby is green because the part of the frosting it was sitting in was green. Since I've started looking at King Cakes at the supermarket I've also seen purple babies and gold babies. It's no accident that this baby is green.

Tradition has it that whoever gets the piece with the baby in it gets to host the next party, at which another King Cake will presumably be served, with another baby, - (or maybe the same baby, baked into the next cake?) etc. This keeps the parties going ad infinitum. Since I got the whole cake, I got the baby. Which means I get to have the next party.

So here's the party I want to have. It's called "Green Baby as Meme." A "meme," according to Richard Dawkins, is an unquestioned idea or thought pattern that, like a gene, passes from one generation to another and, like a germ, passes from one person to another. Assumptions, beliefs, values - all of these are memes and they bind us together into a cohesive society. In his book, *The Selfish Gene,* Dawkins explains that a meme is a chunk of cultural information that sticks. It might be as small as a "where's the beef" commercial, or as large as the notion of reincarnation. When a meme "sticks" it can change the culture in which it occurs.

Most memes are harmless - even useful. They eliminate the need to thoroughly explore every issue before making up our minds about how to behave or what conclusions to draw from our experience. Most memes serve to pass on wisdom and moral behavior. But some memes are malignant. A meme that might have been appropriate at an earlier time, if unquestioned, can be like a virus in the cultural mind; an inappropriate idea that spreads throughout society. A malignant meme can make the culture as a whole sick. The traditional American lawn is such a meme.

As meme, the traditional lawn reflects a larger cultural meme of the Western world, the idea of material progress and heroic advance. This onward and upward view of history carries with it the implication of man's conquest of the natural world - the beating back of the wilderness. The traditional lawn has taken its place as a most exquisite expression of that conquest.

The opposite of a Great Truth is another Great Truth - a profundity that through overuse has collapsed into a cliché. It might likewise be said that the opposite of a Great Meme is another Great Meme. When two memes seem to be in diametric opposition, the situation is ripe for transformation.

Here sits a green baby. It beseeches from my windowsill. It represents something new and green that has just been born. It wants to be picked up, loved, nurtured. I think of this book as a King Cake. Writing it has been an unfolding of my own ecological conscience. It's also been like having a party. Now it's time for the reader to have the next party, and bake the next King Cake. I pass my green baby on to you. Bake it into your cake. Pick it up. Love it. Nurture it. Like any baby, it comes with responsibility and heartache. It won't be easy, loving this baby. But if you do, I guarantee it will bring you joy beyond measure.

APPENDICES

Appendix A: Resources

Appendix B: The Genetic Bill of Rights

Appendix C: Wild Ones Model Municipal Ordinance

Appendix A:

Resources

Landscape Ordinance Research Project: http://www.greenlaws.lsu.edu

Bret Rappaport's article in the *John Marshall Law Review* (Vol. 26, Summer, 1993).

Ladybird Johnson Wildflower Center: http://www.wildflower.org/clearinghouse/articles/Lawns.pdf

Sustainable Sites Initiative: http://www.sustainablesites.org/SustainableSitesInitiative_PreliminaryReport_110107.pdf

Natureserve: A Network Connecting Science with Conservation Providing the scientific basis for effective conservation, NatureServe and its network of natural heritage programs are the trusted source for information about rare and endangered species and threatened ecosystems. http://www.natureserve.org/

Smaller American Lawns Today: http://arboretum.conncoll.edu/salt/salt.html

US Environmental Protection Agency, Green Acres Program: (Weedlaws /Toolkit / Native Vegetation Enhancement / Wild Ones Handbook / Factsheets / Landscaping Naturally (video) (http://www.epa.gov/greenacres/

Wild Ones: Native Plants, Natural Landscapes: http://www.for-wild.org/

Natural Landscaping for Public Officials, available at no cost by writing or calling The Northeast Illinois Planning Commission (312) 454-0400, 222 S. Riverside Plaza, Suite 1800, Chicago, IL 60606

Carolyn McDade, Music about the interdependence of all life: http://www.carolynmcdademusic.com

Rails to Trails Conservancy, promoting a nationwide trail network, using abandoned railroad beds: http://www.railstotrails.org/index.html?gclid=CKC2npuI4ZUCFSASQQodXxILYQ

"Environmentally Friendly Vegetation Management" utlilizing grazing goats: http://goatsrus.com/contact.htm

National Native Plant Nursery Directory:
http://www.plantnative.org/national_nursery_dir_main.htm

Appendix B:

The Genetic Bill of Rights

THE GENETIC BILL OF RIGHTS

by The Board of Directors of the Council for Responsible Genetics

PREAMBLE

Our life and health depend on an intricate web of relationships within the biological and social worlds. Protection of these relationships must inform all public policy.

Commercial, governmental, scientific and medical institutions promote manipulation of genes despite profound ignorance of how such changes may affect the web of life. Once they enter the environment, organisms with modified genes cannot be recalled and pose novel risks to humanity and the entire biosphere.

Manipulation of human genes creates new threats to the health of individuals and their offspring, and endangers human rights, privacy and dignity.

Genes, other constituents of life, and genetically modified organisms themselves are rapidly being patented and turned into objects of commerce. This commercialization of life is veiled behind promises to cure disease and feed the hungry.

People everywhere have the right to participate in evaluating the social and biological implications of the genetic revolution and in democratically guiding its applications.

To protect our human rights and integrity and the biological integrity of the earth, we, therefore, propose this Genetic Bill of Rights.

THE GENETIC BILL OF RIGHTS

1. All people have the right to preservation of the earth's biological and genetic diversity.

2. All people have the right to a world in which living organisms cannot be patented, including human beings, animals, plants, microorganisms and all their parts.

3. All people have the right to a food supply that has not been genetically engineered.

4. All indigenous peoples have the right to manage their own biological resources, to preserve their traditional knowledge, and to protect these from expropriation and biopiracy by scientific, corporate or government interests.

5. All people have the right to protection from toxins, other contaminants, or actions that can harm their genetic makeup and that of their offspring.

6. All people have the right to protection against eugenic measures such as forced sterilization or mandatory screening aimed at aborting or manipulating selected embryos or fetuses.

7.All people have the right to genetic privacy including the right to prevent the taking or storing of bodily samples for genetic information without their voluntary informed consent.

8.All people have the right to be free from genetic discrimination.

9.All people have the right to DNA tests to defend themselves in criminal proceedings.

10.All people have the right to have been conceived, gestated, and born without genetic manipulation.

Spring, 2000
(C) The Council for Responsible Genetics

Appendix C:

Wild Ones Model
Municipal Ordinance

Model Municipal Ordinance

A MODEL MUNICIPAL ORDINANCE ENCOURAGING THE USE OF
NATIVE PLANT COMMUNITIES AS AN ALTERNATIVE IN URBAN
LANDSCAPE DESIGN

The Common Council of the City of _____
_____ do ordain as follows:

SECTION 1. <u>Legislative Purpose</u>: A variety of landscapes adds
diversity and richness to the quality of life in _____
_____. There are, nonetheless, reasonable
expectations regarding the city's landscapes which, if not met,
may decrease the value of nearby properties, degrade the
natural environment, or threaten the public health and safety.
It is therefore in the public interest, and within the purview of
this legislation, to provide standards for the development and
maintenance of the city's landscapes, whether corporate, private,
or public.

The city recognizes the landowners' interest in having managed
turf grass landscapes. At the same time, the city encourages
the preservation, restoration, and management of native plant
communities and wildlife habitats within the city limits. The city
recognizes that the use of wildflowers and other native plants

in managed landscapes is economical, reduces maintenance, effectively conserves water, soil, and other elements of the natural community. Moreover, the preservation, restoration, and management of native plant communities and wildlife habitats may preclude the introduction of toxic pesticides, herbicides, fertilizers, and other pollutants into the environment.

The city further acknowledges the need to enjoy and benefit from the variety, beauty, and practical values of natural landscapes, and seeks to guarantee citizens the freedom to employ varying degrees of natural landscaping as viable and desirable alternatives to other conventional modes of landscaping.

The city seeks to encourage each landowner to create and sustain a condition of ecological stability on his or her land, that is, a state of good health and vigor, as opposed to one of impairment and decline. It is not the intent of this legislation to allow vegetated areas to be unmanaged or overgrown in ways that may adversely affect human health or safety, or pose a threat to agricultural activity. It is the express intent of this city that it shall be lawful to grow native plants, including, but not limited to ferns, grasses, forbs, aquatic plants, trees, and shrubs in a landscape when these plants were obtained not in violation of local, state, or federal laws.

SECTION 2. <u>Definitions</u>: The following terms shall have the stated meanings.
(a) <u>Landowner</u>. One who owns or controls land within the city, including the city itself.
(b) <u>Turf Grass</u>. Grass commonly used in regularly-cut lawns or play areas, such as, but not limited to bluegrass, fescue, and ryegrass blends.
(c) <u>Preservation, or Restoration Area</u>. Any lands managed to preserve or restore native Wisconsin grasses and forbs, native trees, shrubs, wildflowers, and aquatic plants; an oldfield succession of native and non-native plants; or, a combination of these.
(d) <ULWEEDS< u>. The following plant species are defined

as "noxious weeds" under Wisconsin law (66.96, Wis. Stats.): **Cirsium arvense** (Canada thistle); **Convolvulus arvensis** (Field bindweed); **Euphorbia esula** (Leafy spurge). Two species are defined as "nuisance weeds" under Wisconsin law (66.955, Wis. Stats.); **Lythrum salicaria** (Purple loosestrife); **Rosa multiflora** (Multiflora rose). Other particularly invasive, or allergen-producing species such as certain **Arctium spp.** (Burdock), **Cirsium and Carduus spp.** (Thistle), **Ambrosia spp.** (Ragweed), and **Alliaria petiolata** (Garlic mustard), may also be declared as "noxious," or "nuisance" weeds through local legislation.

(e) Destruction: The complete killing of plants, or effectually preventing such plants from maturing to the bloom or flower stage.

SECTION 3. Landowners' Rights and Responsibilities:
(a) This ordinance shall apply equally to all landowners, including the City of _____.
(b) Every landowner having lawns of the conventional turf grass type shall be responsible for managing the turf grass at a height not to exceed inches.
(c) Every landowner shall be responsible for the destruction of all weeds on land which he/she shall own or control.

SECTION 4. Controls. The city may not damage, remove, burn, or cut vegetation of any landowner for which the city does not have management responsibilities, except those species prohibited herein (see SECTION 2, Weeds), and except on order of a court of record following a hearing at which it is established (1) that noxious or nuisance weeds specifically named in the landscape ordinance exist in the landscape; or (2) that a condition creating a clear and present hazard to public health or safety has arisen; or (3) that the condition is a threat to the agricultural economy; or (4) that the conditions of SECTION 3, entitled Landowners' Rights and Responsibilities, have not been met. A court order under these subsections shall provide that the destruction, cutting, or removal of the offending vegetation shall be selective so as not to harm that vegetation which is compliant with the law. In all such cases, the cost of the undertaking shall be attached to the landowner's tax statement. # # # This model ordinance was prepared under the auspices of The Native Plant Preservation Coalition of Wisconsin, in cooperation with the Milwaukee Chapter of the National Audubon Society. Members of the drafting committee were:

Don Vorpahl, Hilbert, WI (Chairman)
Mark Feider, Glendale, WI

Jane Carpenter, Grafton, WI
Lorrie Otto, Bayside, WI

Carol Chew, Bayside, WI
Bret Rappaport, Deerfield, IL, (ad hoc)

Greg David, Watertown, WI
John Vandlik, Milwaukee, WI

Martyn Dibben, Glendale, WI
Rochelle Whiteman, Glendale, WI

ENDNOTES

(Endnotes)

Chapter 1   It Seemed Like a Good Idea at the Time

[1] Cronin, John, and Kennedy, Robert Jr., *The Riverkeepers*, (Scribner & Sons, New York, NY, 1997, p. 140).

[2] IBID., p 141.

[3] Borman, F. Herbert, Balmori, Diana, & Geballe, Gordon T., Vernegaard, Lisa, Ed. *Redesigning the American Lawn: A Search for Environmental Harmony*, (Yale University Press, New Haven & London, 1991 pp. 70-71).

[4] Tharp, Mike, "Lake Tahoe's Clouded Fate," 2/28/01 *U. S. News and World Report.*

[5] Steingraber, Sandra, *Living Downstream*, (Vintage Books (an imprint of Random House) New York, NY, 1998).

[6] Pamphlet: *The New American Lawn*, The Garden Club of America.

[7] Op. Cit., Steingraber, p. 282.

[8] EPA Consumer Factsheet on: 2,4-D.

[9] Op. Cit., Steingraber, p. 96.

[10] IBID., p. 281.

[11] Carbaryl Residues in Bees, Honey, and Bee Bread Following Exposure to Carbaryl Via the Food Supply, Vol 1, # 4 December, 1973 Journal: Archives of Environmental Contamination & Toxology.

[12] Op. Cit., Steingraber, p. 161.

[13] Meyers, Nancy & Sperger, Carloyn, "A Precautionary Primer," Fall, 2001, *Yes! A Journal of Positive Futures.*

[14] "Canadian Government Sued for Banning Lindane," December 10, 2001 *The Globe and Mail;* http://sports.yahoo.com/m/environmental/news/getf/20020122/getfcanadiangovernmentsue.

[15] *The Journal of Pesticide Reform,* Summer, 2006, Vol. 26, No. 2.

[16] Colborn, Theo, Dumanoski, Dianne, & Peterson Myers, John, *Our Stolen Future,* (Penguin Books USA, Inc., New York, NY, 1996, p. 216).

[17] May 11-12, 1996, *The Capitol Times.*

[18] Muschamp, Herbert, "Looking at the Lawn Beneath the Surface," 7/5/98 *New York Times.*

Chapter 2 Lawn Sculpting

[19] Hillman, James, "The Practice of Beauty," in *Uncontrollable Beauty: Toward a New Aesthetics,* Ed: Bill Beckley, with David Shapiro, (Allworth Press, New York, NY, 1998, p. 264).

Chapter 3 Whose Habitat?

[20] Petit, Charles, "Bambi Goes Bicoastal," 12/14/98 *U.S. News and World Report.*

[21] Krier, Al, *Animal Advisory* brochure.

[22] Schechter, Jonathan, "All Nature's Creatures Gravitate to Friendly Habitat," *3/2/02 Oxford Eccentric.*

[23] April, 2000 *EAD Bulletin,* the newsletter of the Michigan Retired Engineer Technical Assistance Program (RETAP).

[24] Flocke, Jeff, "Keep the Wild Alive," National Wildlife Federation Spring, 2000 *Habitats.*

[25] Op. Cit., Flocke.

Chapter 4 Where the Wild Things Are

[26] Dubos, Rene', *The Wooing of Earth: New Perspectives on Man's Use of Nature,* (Charles Scribner & Sons, New York, NY, 1980 p. 113).

Chapter 5 Native Plants

[27] Jensen, Jens, *Siftings,* (Johns Hopkins University Press, Baltimore/London, 1939, p.21).

[28] For an excellent discussion of gene-heterogeneity vs. gene-pollution, see "Genetically Speaking", by Bill Schneider, at http://www.msu.edu/user/widltype/gentalkhtm.

[29] *Natural Landscaping for Public Officials: A Source Book,* prepared by the Northeastern Illinois Planning Commission, Second Printing, 1998, p. 61.

Chapter 6 Planning, Planting, Maintaining

[30] Ann Arbor, Michigan Parks and Recreation brochure.

Chapter 7 Alien Invasions

[31] "Biodiversity Imperiled," May/June 2000 *Nature Conservancy.*

[32] Wolfe, Joanne, "The Joy of Wild Gardening," (Vol. 1 *Wild Garden*).

[33] Ann Arbor Parks and Recreation brochure.

[34] Russell, Peter, *Waking Up in Time*, Harper, San Francisco, 1998.

[35] Truxil, John, Quoted in "Mammals, Fish, Birds, Amphibians, Reptiles Suffering Major Declines", May 21, 1998 Worldwatch Institute news release.

[36] Pollan, Michael, *Second Nature: A Gardener's Education*, (Dell Publishing, New York, NY 1991, p. 115).

[37] July, Aug., 2000 *Nature Conservancy.*

Chapter 8 Vegetative Warfare
(no endnotes)

Chapter 9 Learning Curve

[38] Hayden, Thomas, "Bad Seeds in Court", January 28/February 4, 2002 *U.S. News and world Report.*

[39] IBID.

[40] Mellon, Margaret, & Rissler, Jeanne, "Caterpillar in a Coal Mine," Summer, 2000 *Nucleus.*

[41] Milstein, Sarah, "Genetically Modified Foods," March/April, 2000 *Natural HOME.*

[42] IBID.

[43] IBID.

[44] IBID.

[45] Vajhala, Surekha, "Of Luscious lawns and Lavender Lilies," August 14, 2000 *U.S. News and World Report.*

[46] "Biodiversity Imperiled," May/June, 2000 *Nature Conservancy.*

[47] Pollan, Michael, "The Pesticide Potato," Spring, 2000 *Greenprints.*

[48] Simmons, Phillip E., "Wild Things," (December, 1998 *World*).

Chapter 10 Jens Jensen: Native Landscape Prophet

[49] Grese, Robert E , Jens *Jensen: Maker of Natural Parks and Gardens*, (The Johns Hopkins University Press, Baltimore & London, 1992, p. 2).

[50] IBID. p. 5.

[51] Jensen, Jens, *Siftings*, (Johns Hopkins University Press, Baltimore, and London, 1939, 1990 edition, p. 34.

[52] Lima, Patrick with Scanlan, John (PHT), *The Art of Perennial Gardening*, Firefly Books, Richmond Hill, Ontario, Canada, 1998. p. 42.

[53] Op Cit, Grese, p. 8.

[54] Jensen and Eskil, "Natural Parks and Gardens," *The Saturday Evening Post*, Vol. 202, no. 36, (March 8, 1930, p. 19).

[55] Op. Cit., Grese, p. 45.

[56] W. Miller 1915, *The Prairie Spirit in Landscape Gardening*, pp. 33-34.

[57] Op. Cit., Grese, p. 59.

[58] Op. Cit., Grese, p. 160.

Chapter 11 Lasting Impacts

[59] IBID. p. 109.

[60] IBID.p. 130.

[61] IBID.p. 124.

[62] IBID. p. 76.

[63] IBID.p. 114.

[64] July/August 2000 *Nature Conservancy.*

[65] IBID.

[66] Op. Cit., Grese, p. 94.

[67] IBID.

Chapter 12 A New Lawn Aesthetic

[68] Briggs, John, *Fractals: The Patterning of Chaos*, (Simon & Schuster, New York, NY, 1992, p. 90).

[69] IBID. p. 115.

Chapter 13 A Fractal Approach

[70] IBID, p 158.

[71] Op. Cit., Grese, P. 59.

[72] IBID, p. 147.

[73] IBID, p. 137.

[74] Mills, Stephanie, *In Service of the Wild*, (Beacon Press, Boston, MA, 1995, p.137).

[75] Op. Cit., Briggs, p. 102.

[76] Pollan, Michael, *Second Nature: A Gardener's Education*, (Dell Publishing, New York, NY 1991, p. 5).

[77] Op. Cit., Briggs, p. 158.

[78] IBID, p. 164.

Chapter 14 Heritage Garden

[79] IBID, p. 138.

[80] IBID, p. 163.

[81] IBID p. 164.

[82] IBID. p. 180.

Chapter 15 A Druid in Downtown Detroit

[83] Rappaport, Bret, and Wasowski, Andy, "The Truth About Weed Laws," *The American Gardener*, (May, June, 1998).

[84] IBID.

[85] Aldo Leopold, Dedication Ceremony of the University of Wisconsin Arboretum – 1934.

Chapter 16 What Will The Neighbors Think?
(no endnotes)

Chapter 17 When the Neighbors Get Restless About the Natives

[86] *Wild Ones: Natural Landscapers*, Box 1274, Appleton, WE 54912-1274, www.for-wild.org .

[87] *Natural Landscaping for Public Officials: A Source Book*, (see Appendix C: Model Municipal Ordinance).

[88] IBID.

[89] "Taking P2 Home," April 2000 *EAD Bulletin*.

[90] IBID.

[91] IBID.

Chapter 18 Hummingbird Ridge

[92] Gross, Bob, "Housing Project Putting Emphasis on Preservation," 3/23/00 *Oakland Press.*

[93] Bingham, Marjorie, *Flora of Oakland County, Michigan: A Study in Physiographic Plant Ecology, Bulletin No. 22,* Cranbrook Institute of Science, May, 1945.

[94] *Natural Landscaping for Public Officials: A Source Book*, (Prepared by Northeastern Illinois Planning Commission, Second printing, 1998, p. 4).

[95] The model used was *Model Development Principles,* published by the Center for Watershed Protection.

Chapter 19 Zooming Out

[96] Sometimes these open spaces are given over to private golf courses, in which case you do have a very large lawn. Golf courses are notoriously bad for the environment, with the excessive use of fertilizers, pesticides and watering required to keep them green and smooth. They are "artificially created terrains that have already altered weather patterns and water quality." (from the MSU Turf Grass Program brochure) However, this need no longer be the case. Both the Audubon Society and Michigan State University offer *Turf Grass Programs* to encourage golf course management practices that preserve wildlife habitat and utilize native natural landscaping. This concept is now being modified as a model in Southeastern Michigan for an innovative "Eco-lawn" program in which landscapers can be certified.

[97] IBID., p. 20.

[98] IBID.

99 Rails to Trails, (RTC), a conservancy which is creating a nationwide network of trails from former rail lines and connecting corridors to build healthier places for healthier people, opened its doors February 7, 1986. RTC is headquartered in Washington, D.C. with regional offices in California (Western Region), Ohio (Midwestern Region) and Pennsylvania (Northeastern Region), and a state office in Florida. RTC has helped create nearly 13,935 miles of rail-trails. RTC Website: http://www.railtrails.org/whoweare/index.html.

[99] IBID.

[100] Pepper, John, "Environmental Architect to lead Rouge makeover," Oct. 17, 1999 *Detroit News and Free Press.*

Chapter 20 A New Lawn Philosophy

[101] Muschamp, Herbert, "Looking at the Lawn and Below the Surface," (7/5/98 *New York times).*

103 Rappaport, Bret and Wasonwski, Andy, "The Truth About Weed Laws," *The American Gardener,* (May, June, 1998).

[102] Tarnass, Richard, "The Great Initiation," *Noetic sciences Review,* No. 47.

[103] Op. Cit., Tarnass.

[104] Dobos, Rene', *The Wooing of Earth: New perspectives on Man's Use of Nature,* (Charles Scribner Sons, New York, NY, 1980, p. 143).

[105] IBID.

[106] American Eagle Foundation, www.eagles.org.

[107] Whitman, David, "It's a Breath of Fresh air," April 17, 2000 *U.S. News and World Report.*

[108] Wilson, E. O. "A New Chapter: Saving America's Landmarks," May/June, 2000, *Nature Conservancy.*

[109] Jensen. Jens, *Siftings,* (Johns Hopkins University Press, Baltimore/ London, 1939, p. 27).

Chapter 21 Frog Pond
(no End Notes)

Chapter 22 Conclusion: A Green Baby

[110] Russel, Peter, *Waking Up in Time,* (Origin Press, Inc., Novarto, CA, 1992, p. 111).

[111] Leopold, Aldo, *A Sand County Almanac: With Essays on Conservation from Round River* (Ballantine Books, New York, NY, 1974, p. 262).